Prophets: 101

Jonathan Ferguson
Foreword by: Dr. Paula Price

Copyright © 2013 Jonathan Ferguson
All rights reserved.

ISBN: 1483989712
ISBN-13: 9781483989716

Contents

Foreword by Dr. Paula Price   xi

Chapter One: The Prophetic Call   1
- Understand the process of preparation connected to the prophetic calling
- Understand the stages of development in the call of the prophet
- Understand how to properly answer the call to be a prophet
- Understand why discipleship and training are necessary for those called to the prophetic
- Understand the process of ordination into ministry that Jesus Himself patterned
- Understand the differences between a false prophet and presumptuous prophet

Chapter Two: Office of the Prophet   15
- Learn four spheres of the prophetic
- Understand the correlation between the prophetic mantle and the prophetic office
- Understand the differences between the gift of prophecy and the prophetic mantle

- Understand what the prophetic mantle is and what it represents
- Understand the expanded abilities of one who operates in the prophetic office/mantle

Chapter Three: Defining the Role of the Prophet 27
- Learn three basic things to consider when defining the role of the prophet
- Understand why it's important to study Hebraic definitions of the word "prophet"
- Learn the prophet's role as an officer
- Learn the prophet's role in shifting atmospheres, altering spiritual climates, and manifesting the supernatural
- Learn three dynamics of the "seer" in scripture
- Learn how the seer's anointing & the Issachar anointing connect
- Learn the prophet's role as a gatekeeper and guardian

Chapter Four: History of the Prophet 45
- Review the primary functions of various historical prophets
- Learn why the School of the Prophets was established

- Learn what basic prophetic abilities and anointing come under the prophet's schooling
- Learn why prayer and evangelism are unavoidable fundamentals in the life of the prophet
- Learn what it means for a prophet to function in full capacity

Chapter Five: The Authority of the Prophet   65
- Learn what distinguishes the authority of the prophet
- Learn four things that distinguish the words of a prophet
- Learn how the content of prophecy centers around a prophet's jurisdictional authority
- Learn how prophets expand and broaden the scope and measure of their authority

Chapter Six: The Shift   75
- Understand historically how the life of Samuel correlates with the current shift in the prophetic
- Embrace a shift in the maturity and integrity of the prophetic
- Understand why it is important to begin understanding the prophetic from a Kingdom perspective

Chapter Seven: The Prophet, World Systems, & Kingdom Dynamics   83
- Learn multiple dynamics of the Kingdom
- Understand the Kingdom mandate and the role of the prophet in executing it
- Understand world systems, various kingdoms of this world, and the mandate of the prophet to align them with the Kingdom of God
- Begin to understand the cultural impact of the prophet

Chapter Eight: Culture & Prophetic Systems   91
- Understand the world we live in
- Discover the origin of world systems and various spheres of culture
- Learn what a prophetic system is, when it originated, and its three main historical pillars within Israel's culture
- Continue to understand the cultural impact of the prophet historically

Chapter Nine: Shifting Power Systems   103
- Understand what power shifts are and how prophets initiate them
- Understand the importance of the supernatural in the ministry of the prophet
- Understand how God causes governmental authorities to submit to the counsel of the

- prophets when major shifts need to take place
- Begin to understand how prophets deal with demonic principalities and powers and how prophets must follow up afterward in order to maintain victory

Chapter Ten: Emerging Leaders   **115**
- Understand the importance of next-generation leaders emerging after cultures are altered prophetically
- Cross-reference the current prophetic movement with the confrontation of Elijah against Ahab and Jezebel
- Understand the stages and dangers of moral decline
- Understand Jezebel's lineage, the origin of the Babylonian system, how world systems began to be demonically influenced, and how it all parallels to our current culture
- Understand how the spiritual climate in the eras of Elijah, Noah, and Daniel parallel
- Understand generational breakthroughs and how prophets conquer demonic principalities and powers
- Understand changing times and how all believers play a part in prophetically reforming cultures

Foreword for Prophets 101

Undertaking the treatment to the prophetic today is a bold step. By now one would think that all or most of what can be said on the ministry has been said. But, that would be a mistake and *Prophets 101* proves it. This book gives newcomers and trainers an excellent orientation to the prophetic. And, it is quite useful for those who want to refresh themselves on the ministry. Jonathan Ferguson has impressively delivered broad-based teaching on prophets and the prophetic that immediately enlightens their spiritual and ministerial understanding. What every young prophet must know in order to grab hold of this ministry is in this book. Not only does he brilliantly capture its core attitudes and actions, but `he does so from highly impactful vantage points.

Prophets 101 addresses the primary and essential ideas of prophetic service simply but profoundly. In it, Jonathan makes the prophetic's most difficult and obscure theories graspable and doable. For example, the way he frames his insights on prophetic history, giftings, office, and mantle more than informs or instructs his readers; it equips them, which is the goal of all good writing. His approach gives prophetic trainers and educators who have the privilege of ushering new ministers into this ministry, whether to the gift or the office, an effective tool to use to do so. Almost effortlessly they can adapt this work to their existing courses and use it as a main textbook. Also, this work will appeal to prophetic teachers who will find its easy-to-read yet richly articulated wisdom well suits their developmental ends. The book's core knowledge prepares its readers for more advanced study of this subject.

Lastly, Christians in general could read *Prophets 101* and learn much from it. Many of them will discern it better equips them to judge prophetic service and value its advantage to the Lord and His church. Those who have dreaded or avoided the prophetic because of its lack of clarity can take comfort in the answers this book provides. For these reasons, the book serves as a guardian and guide to ministers and believers alike. As a result, those who honestly embrace its counsel will be more inclined to cooperate with the true prophets the Lord sends their way.

I heartily commend Jonathan for the superb job he has done of effectively condensing the major ideas and functions of prophetic ministry and applaud the sobering way he illuminates the elementary but nonetheless invaluable principles of prophetic service and governance. Finally, his insightful tempering of its most attractive aspects with the awesome responsibilities that ensures its success. Congratulations, Jonathan, on a job well done. God bless you.

Dr. Paula A. Price
Author of *The Prophet's Dictionary* and
The Prophet's Handbook

Chapter 1
The Prophetic Calling

Chapter Objectives:
- Understand the process of preparation connected to the prophetic calling
- Understand the stages of development in the call of the prophet
- Understand how to` properly answer the call to be a prophet
- Understand why discipleship and training are necessary for those called to the prophetic
- Understand the process of ordination into ministry that Jesus Himself patterned
- Understand the differences between a false prophet and presumptuous prophet

The world of prophetics is extremely beyond what is traditionally understood. It is immensely powerful, awe-strikingly profound, and yet unbelievably practical. Make no mistake about it. Prophets are those who are called by God to officiate this world of reality. But everyday people are those who called by God to benefit from it.

Jonathan Ferguson

Prophets or not, it is time we all had better understanding of the vast extent of how God designed and purposed the prophet to function. Whether you are newly called, well experienced, or *not even called at all* as a prophet, this book will undoubtedly serve as a must-have resource in your library. There is so much you will learn about the prophet as you read this book that it is literally going to blow your mind. However, in the process of doing so, it's important you first somewhat understand the process of preparation that is connected to the calling.

Truth is, in order to truly enjoy and benefit from the prophetic, there must be a healthy respect for the ministry of the prophet. And one of the things that will help us maintain or acquire a healthy respect for the prophet is to understand that the ministry of the prophet is not something that an individual steps into overnight. This is why I named this chapter, "The Prophetic Call." In it, I want to discuss not merely the call, but more so the preparation that must take place after an individual becomes aware he or she is indeed called by God as a prophet.

This is by far not an exhaustive writing concerning the preparation process of the prophet, yet it will yet suffice as a foundation prior to us exploring the prophet's office. In fact, by the time you complete the entire book, this particular chapter would have become of even greater significance. You will find that the more aware you become of the many facets pertaining to who prophets are and what all they are called to do, the more you will likewise understand the necessity of such individuals being properly prepared to function in that calling.

Why Prophets 101?

Many people grossly underestimate the preparation necessary to function in maximum capacity of their prophetic calling. This is error and should be corrected if prophetic potential is to be fully developed. For example, I have had many individuals tell me that they were called to be a prophet from their mother's womb. The only problem is they fail to understand that such an acknowledgement doesn't exclude them from discipleship.

Prophets are not born; they are made. When an individual recognizes the call of the prophet on his life, the proper way to answer the call is to embrace adequate teaching, training, and coaching. Therefore, acknowledging the call to be a prophet is only the beginning of the process it takes in order to mature in such a calling.

There is a weighty responsibility to the prophet's office that God does not entrust to individuals who have not been proven. Israel's historical prophetic culture is a great example of this truth. The significance and credentials of the office were well respected and recognized no less than any other profession.

Jonathan Ferguson

There were multiple schools of the prophets represented throughout Israel's history that served as training facilities for budding prophets. Therein, prophets were able to receive adequate teaching, training, and even a type of internship experience. I'm going to take time to explain the school of the prophets in more detail to you in upcoming chapters. However, for now we should understand that if the prophets of this hour will be as effective as the prophets of old were, we must return back to the school of the prophets, which is why I call this book *Prophets 101*.

Answering the Call

There are different stages of developing in the call of the prophet that begins with either an awareness of that call or an awakening of prophetic abilities. These are two different factors—both equally important in the process of beginning the developmental progression into the ministry of the prophet. For example, there are individuals who have prophetic ability from God, but they do not have the call of the prophet on their lives. In other words, although they can prophesy, they are yet not called to be prophets. In the next chapter, we will clarify why the ability to prophesy is not the only criterion that qualifies an individual to be a prophet. For now, let's continue to understand the stages of becoming aware of prophetic abilities and answering the prophetic call

The awareness of the prophetic call comes at different times for different people. It comes for some at a young age, for others at salvation, or after they receive the infilling of the Holy Spirit. On the contrary, for many there is an awakening of prophetic abilities prior to their awareness of the call. In fact, in such cases among those who have had prophetic abilities awakened prior to understanding the call, there have been many who have ended up mishandling the prophetic. They often become false prophets, psychics, active in dark arts, or sadly, just simply individuals who never maximize the call of God on their lives. In whatever way the initial introduction to the prophetic begins, the calling of God stands sure, yet few recognize and answer the call properly.

The Called and The Chosen

The bible teaches that many are called yet few are chosen. The problem is that many are yet to discern the difference between when God calls them into ministry, and when He actually chooses for them to be active in that ministry. In most cases, if an individual accepts their calling into ministry and goes through some type of ordination process, we feel as if that validates them for the ministry to which they feel called. I have discovered that this is rather different than the process that Jesus instituted in choosing His apostles in Mark 3:13-15. In fact, I believe that Mark 3:13-15 should once again be the pattern of New Testament ministerial appointments. Let's briefly take a look at the ordination process that Jesus Himself instituted.

Jesus' Process of Ministerial Recruitment

Notice in Mark 3:13-15 the progression into ministry is that the apostles were first called and ordained to be with Jesus. However, I'm convinced that many have confused this process with being called into the ministry and ordained to preach. In fact, many are yet to understand that the callings on our lives extend far beyond the calling of the prophet or any other ministry gifts. In Mark 3:13-15, the scripture does not say that Jesus called them into the ministry, but that He called them and He ordained that they be with Him. Lastly, it was only after being with Jesus that He not only sent them to preach, but also to have power to heal the sick and cast out devils.

Although the preaching and the power is wonderful, I believe the most important part of Mark 3:13-15 that many overlook is how Jesus ordained the twelve to *be with him*. In other words, this is what it truly means to be ordained. It's not about receiving the credentials of man, or the endorsement of a particular denomination. It's always been and always will be about being with Jesus in His presence. We have to find a way to embrace this reality and make it our highest priority. And whenever starting a ministry becomes more important than an individual's relationship with the Lord Jesus, it should be evident that the individual esteems being ordained by man over being validated by heaven.

Bottom line, Mark 3:13-15 is what those who are called to the prophetic must return to. After all, the spirit of prophecy is the testimony of Jesus (Revelations 19:10). There are far too many who desire to be prophetic, yet have no true desire to be closer to Jesus. This is backwards and must change. In fact, when we teach people how to be close to Jesus, we don't have to teach them how to hear God and prophesy as much because they would learn to know Him and as they do, the prophetic would be inevitable.

It is also important that we also know according to Mark 3:13-15 that whenever Jesus "called" an individual to Himself, there was a process of discipleship and preparation initiated. In fact, the individuals who were called by Jesus were actually known as His disciples before they were recognized in their ministry calling as Apostles. It is as they were ordained to be with Jesus, that He personally trained them and eventually commissioned them, sending them out to preach in His name with power.

Let me make this plain and simple. If an individual does not show forth the power of what they claim to be called to, it is because they have not been sent by Jesus. If they have not been sent by Jesus, it is because they have not been spending time with Him. If they have not been spending time with Jesus, it is because they are not truly called.

Called & Commissioned

It is a great acknowledgement to know that you are called to be a prophet. However, the problem is the majority of individuals believe that the extent of them acknowledging their calling means that they get to add a title to their name. My response is always that the awareness that an individual is called to be a prophet is only the beginning of the training process.

In fact, discipleship should always follow the call of the prophet. Just because a person is aware that they are called as a prophet does not mean that they are ready to function in the office of the prophet. This is why 2 Timothy 4:5 instructs us to make full proof of our ministry.

There are many who operate in the prophetic who have been called to the prophetic, but they not been commissioned in the prophetic. They don't have heaven's reinforcing power and authority because they have not been authenticated as of yet. Even Isaiah the prophet prophesied six chapters before he was actually sent by God (Isaiah 6:1-8).

The difference is that when the Lord Jesus actually sends and commissions someone into the call of the prophet, they are no longer operating by mere zeal or passion. The burden of the Lord rests on them and they are held responsible for the ministry they have been given.

In other words, once the Lord actually commissions an individual, it is serious business. They no longer have a choice; they must comply and they must prophesy or innocent blood will be required at their hands. The prophetic office is not for those who are merely practicing prophecy. There are very important matters concerning the office of the prophet that the Lord requires one to understand prior to receiving His commission.

The Lord will not prematurely qualify an individual for the office of the prophet no more than a hospital will allow a nurse to perform brain surgery. Although the nurse is in the medical field, he or she not qualified as a surgeon. It would be just as questionable for an individual who is gifted and called to the prophetic to function in the office of the prophet unprepared.

There are many reading this now and you are either called to the prophetic office or you are confused about the whole matter of the prophetic maybe because of some negative experiences with some who claim to have operated as prophets. You are one of the reasons that the Spirit of God led me to write this book. We have to understand that when a person has not properly answered his or her call to the prophetic,

Jonathan Ferguson

and attempts to operate prematurely in the prophetic, it causes confusion for everyone involved.

Others of you are reading this book because you need a more holistic understanding of who God has called you to be as a prophet. The remainder of you are likely reading this book because you need God to redefine in your life what the prophetic truly is or you just want to have a deeper understanding of the it. Whoever you may be and whatever stage you are in pertaining to your walk with Jesus, this book is for you.

False Prophet or Presumptuous Prophet

Before you conclude this introductory chapter, I think it is very important that you understand one of the biggest misconceptions concerning the Prophet. The misconception is that we often consider a person who is immature in their calling to be a false prophet while individuals who are in actuality false prophets, we often validate as true prophets because of their level of gifting. In order to clear the misconception, we must understand that there is a difference between a false prophet and a presumptuous prophet. The mystery within this difference is that a false prophet will often also be presumptuous, yet a presumptuous prophet is not necessarily false.

A prophet who is presumptuous is primarily one who is immature in the calling. They speak of their own initiative and have not been authorized to speak on behalf of God. I'm sure there are many other meanings of such a person; however, this is the portion that I am called to reveal. Notice in Deuteronomy 18:20-22 how even God acknowledges such a person's call to the prophetic, and because of this, the misconceptions must be cleared up.

What makes a prophet a prophet is not merely whether prophecies come to pass or not, neither is it based on how much they may prophesy. If an individual prophesies something that does not come to pass, it could simply mean that they have prophesied presumptuously or they just missed it. However, even if a person speaks a thing and it comes to pass, yet their character is not valid or if they lead individuals away from Jesus, that person is a false prophet (Deuteronomy 13:1-5; Matthew 7:15-23).

However, there are those who are authentically called to the office of the prophet, yet they are not as sharp in their prophetic abilities or they are operating by their own initiative. This person is a presumptuous prophet. After all, it is expected for one to be immature in the prophetic if there has been no training. This is one reason why a person should not assume that the awareness of their call or mere prophetic ability or gifting gives them the license to function in that calling.

Its time we stop labeling the presumptuous as false prophets and the false prophets as true prophets. It is important you learn to adequately determine

Jonathan Ferguson

what is what and who is who, and this book is going to help you in the process. By the time you finish reading, you will understand who the prophet is, what they are called to do, and why that is significant in your life whether you are called to be a prophet or not.

Although the prophet is under scrutiny as never before, the standard of authentic prophetic expression is simultaneously being raised. I truly believe the body of Christ is returning to what the prophetic was originally purposed to represent. However, in the process we should have some guidelines.

For one, we should not be so quick to endorse the ministry of the prophet in an individual who has not been proven. Likewise, we shouldn't be so quick to validate a prophet as false either. We should rather give ourselves in understanding what the role of the prophet biblically consists of. We should then take what we have learned and thoroughly examine the one that claims to be a prophet prior to determining whether they are authentic, presumptuous, or false.

There are several types of individuals reading this book right now. Some of you have been disgusted by even the mentioning of the prophetic because of those who have established entire ministries in either mere gifting, falsehood, or presumption. There are also some of you who know that you are called to the prophetic and desire mentorship, or maybe even you simply desire to know more about the prophetic.

Whatever the case may be, I pray this book becomes a measuring rod by which you can discern the real from the counterfeit and begin to understand one of the Lord's most powerful officers who establishes His Kingdom in the earth. Welcome to Prophets 101; Class in now in session.

Chapter 2
Office of the Prophet

Chapter Objectives:
- Learn four spheres of the prophetic
- Understand the correlation between the prophetic mantle and the prophetic office
- Understand the differences between the gift of prophecy and the prophetic mantle
- Understand what the prophetic mantle is and what it represents
- Understand the expanded abilities of one who operates in the prophetic office/mantle

The Gift vs. The Mantle

There are four basic spheres of the prophetic: the gift of prophecy, the spirit of prophecy, Bible prophecy, and the office of the prophet. The gift of prophecy can be found in 1 Corinthians 12:10. The spirit of prophecy can be found in Revelations 19:10. Bible prophecy is found in 2 Peter 1:20-21, and the office of the prophet is found in Ephesians 4:11.

Out of the four spheres, the gift of prophecy and the spirit of prophecy are actually sub units of the prophetic office. Each sphere is multi-dimensional, consisting of multiple factors. For example, in 1 Corinthians

Jonathan Ferguson

14:3, we learn that the gift of prophecy comes for the purposes of comfort, edification, and exhortation. It is very clear according to 1 Corinthians 14:3 that this one sphere of the prophetic is of itself multifaceted. The other spheres of the prophetic are no less multi-dimensional, especially when dealing with the office of the prophet.

A book could probably be written on each sphere separately; however, my assignment in this book is not to expound on such. In this book I want to deal strictly with the office of the prophet. My goal is that you more clearly understand what being a prophet is all about, but for more information concerning the other spheres of the prophetic, I recommend my book entitled *Experiencing God in the Supernatural*. Pastor Benny Hinn also has great audio/video teaching on the four various spheres of the prophetic.

A Basic in Understanding the Office

There is a huge misunderstanding concerning the role of the prophet due to a lack of understanding the prophet's office versus the gift of prophecy. Therefore, we must acknowledge the basic difference between a person operating in the gift of prophecy and a person operating in the office of the prophet. The basic premise is that a prophet will always have the ability to operate in the gift of prophecy; however, a person's ability to operate in the gift of prophecy does not always mean that he or she occupies the office of the prophet.

Prophets: 101

When a person is operating in the office of a prophet, there is a prophetic mantle in operation causing his or her capabilities to be extended beyond the basic functions of the gift of prophecy. In fact, most of the prophets in scripture operated very little in the gift of prophecy in comparison to how they functioned in their mantles. For this reason it is important to take a moment and examine what the prophetic mantle entails.

What is the Prophet's Mantle?

A mantle was simply a cloak. The word "mantle" is literally an old English word used to describe an outer garment. It was a piece of clothing that the prophet wore that distinguished the nature of the prophetic anointing that they carried in the eyes of the people. It could pass as something like a prophet's uniform, and the nature of the clothing would often be symbolic of something that was very supernatural in nature.

In fact, the way the prophets dressed, the way they carried themselves, and even where they lived was prophetic to the nature of their purpose and assignment. However, in today's world, the prophet's mantle is no longer something that is material and physically worn as clothing. In the Old Testament, the mantle was only a type and shadow of what is now given to the prophet to function as a prophet through the power of the Holy Ghost. Therefore, when we talk

Jonathan Ferguson

about the mantle, we are speaking of what it spiritually represents.

What does the Mantle Represent?

The scriptures teach that we are endued with power in Luke 24:49, and that we receive power as the Holy Ghost comes upon us in Acts 1:8. The word "endued" literally means to be clothed. This means that when the Holy Ghost comes on us, our "dress code" changes in the Spirit realm. The scriptures confirm this as they speak about our spiritual apparel that includes the armor of God and more (Ephesians 6:11; Romans 13:14; Revelations 3:18).

I reiterate that the word "mantle" is merely an old English word used to describe an outer garment. It is a natural word that represents a spiritual thing. The mantle represents the Spirit of God on people to anoint them for what they are called to do. The mantle was something that the prophet wore in the natural that is symbolic of how God clothes us by His spirit so that when people look at us, they don't see us, but they see the anointing. Therefore, the term mantle can be used interchangeably with the term office in reference to the anointing and grace on a person who is called to the official position of the prophet.

The Prophet's Mantle

When the scriptures talk about being clothed in power in Luke 24:49, it is talking about the power of the mantle. It is the Spirit of God that covers our flesh and empowers us so that we are not moving in our own personal power or strength. This is why Jesus said that the Spirit of the Lord was on Him to anoint Him in Luke 4:18, because we cannot be clothed with power unless the Spirit of God is on us. He was talking about His mantle.

The previous is very key because there are different mantles for different callings, and different anointings for different mantles. In other words, if we are called we have a mantle, and if we have a mantle, there should be various anointings that accompany that mantle. Notice in Luke 4:18-19, it was only after Jesus talked about the Spirit being on Him that the scripture then goes on to note various specific abilities because of the anointing.

The same is true with every mantle in that it is validated by various anointings that are assigned to it. In fact, if we are using Luke 4:18-19 as a pattern, we understand that there should be multiple and not just one type of anointing that accompanies the mantle. Likewise, the mantle of the prophet would have to equip one in the office of the prophet to accomplish multiple tasks beyond prophesying. We will expound upon the various anointings that should accompany the mantle of the prophet over the next couple of chapters.

How to Distinguish Gift from Mantle

The powers and abilities of the prophetic mantle extend beyond spoken prophecy, although the gift of prophecy remains a key component within the prophet's office. A great way to distinguish the gift from the mantle or office is very simple. The gift will always have more of a verbal function. However, the office or mantle will have multiple functions that are beyond the spoken word of prophecy.

In fact, when the mantle of the prophet is functioning, there will always be a corporate impact for multiple individuals collectively. The gift of prophecy changes lives primarily one by one. However, the mantle of the prophet can birth, transform, deliver, heal, and prosper whole nations at once. The mantle or office of the prophet is by far more holistic in its operation than the gift of prophecy.

A person who walks in the office of the prophet is mantled so that his authority is uniformed and recognized in the realm of the spirit. They are mantled so that they can cover more ground and get more done than someone who will only prophesy to individuals one by one. When a prophet is operating in the mantle, they don't necessarily have to prophesy. The weight of their mantle can be felt without them having to open their mouths.

Corporate Impact of the Prophet

If we are going to understand the office of the prophet, we have to take the time to distinguish the difference between the personal impact of prophecy versus the corporate impact of the prophetic mantle. Although corporate prophecy has an element of impact, we should understand how there is a corporate impact of the prophet that extends beyond even corporate prophecy.

Abraham is a great example of how a prophet can have a corporate impact beyond the spoken word of prophecy. Although he was not a "worldwide" evangelist, scriptures say that he was a friend of God, and Jesus said of Abraham that he was a prophet. An interesting fact, however, is that we do not see Abraham functioning in the prophetic according to what is typically understood about the prophetic. Abraham's primary prophetic calling was to prayer and we see him functioning in such as he intercedes for Sodom.

This is a rather different perspective of what we consider to be prophetic. Many in today's church culture probably would not have considered Abraham as a prophet because of how Abraham functioned in his prophetic mantle. It is not recorded that Abraham ever released a spoken prophecy. However, he knew the

Jonathan Ferguson

thing that would come to pass in Sodom while actually dwelling at a completely different location in the plains of Mamre (Genesis 18:16-18). This is powerful because it not only verifies that the Lord would speak to Abraham, but also that God had given him regional prophetic authority that extended beyond his geographical location. This would be likened to if I lived in Africa, yet God included me in the behind-the-scenes counsel meeting in heaven concerning what is to take place in China.

Abraham's life is evidence that the prophetic capacity that is developed in prayer extends far beyond spoken prophecy. However, there are many "so called prophets" who only desire to have public ministry success while remaining private failures in their prayer lives. Abraham was not an itinerate prophet traveling from city to city prophesying in conferences and revival services. The goal of his ministry was not to call out names and bank account numbers, although there is nothing wrong with that.

It was as Abraham interceded, even though he never released a public prophetic word, that he knew the thing that was to come to pass in Sodom. His success as a prophet was based on how close he was to God. So that whenever God wanted to manifest something divine or avert something demonic in the earth, the Lord could count on Abraham to intercede.

More than a Gift -- More than Prophecy

Abraham's protocol and responsibility as a prophet was not to go announce a prophetic message to Sodom. In fact, as a friend, there was a level of confidentiality required. However, his mantle was so powerful that people were able to benefit from the prophetic anointing on his life without him even having to prophesy.

It was because of the prophetic anointing on Abraham's life that angels were sent into Sodom to save Lot and his family from destruction. This is powerful because not only did Abraham *not* prophesy, but also his prayers were *not* directed towards Lot and his family. I believe this demonstrates the power of how prophetic intercession can impact regions and the people of that region. A prophet does not need to pray for everyone's personal prayer request; however, everyone connected to the prophet can be blessed every time that prophet begins to pray. When a prophet prays, things can begin to turn and be shifted in people's favor.

Is there a Prophet among you?

When Abraham prayed for Sodom, even though Sodom was not saved, there were those that were saved out of Sodom. This is significant because there are many things that seem to happen unexpectedly and people often ask where are the prophets. What

Jonathan Ferguson

they don't know is that even though there was not an open warning of certain disaster, God was able to send angelic intervention for individuals to avert the impending destruction because there was a prophet interceding.

For example, there are testimonies of those who never showed up to work or got on their flights during the September 11th attack on the twin towers. I believe such testimonies were the result of prophetic intercession and angelic intervention. I'm not at all teaching that only prophets can be this effective in prayer; however, I am stating that this should definitely be active in the lives of individuals who walk in the office of the prophet.

There is another interesting factor about Abraham's encounter with God concerning Sodom. Pay very close attention to this because there is a powerful revelation of the prophet's mantle revealed here. The scriptures teach that after the angels visited Abraham, they were then sent to rescue Lot and his family out of Sodom.

Now in order to get the revelation you have to notice that Abraham was not sent to Sodom, although it was his prayer that saved Lot and his family from the impending destruction of Sodom. In other words, God had assigned angels to Lot and his family because of the anointing on Abraham's life. However, it then became Lot's assignment to get his family out of Sodom. This means that when Lot had the angelic encounter in Sodom, it was like a baton was being passed to him, which began with Abraham.

Now hear is the revelation. As prophets, there are some things that will begin with us in private and in the secret place that others in different parts of the world will pick up the mandate and assignment for publicly. There are ministries that would not have a public voice right now if it were not for some of the prophets that are still hidden in prayer. This means that when God begins to raise up new leadership and new voices in the body of Christ, it is a sign that there is a prophet among us.

Although we will expound on more concerning the prophet, the corporate impact of the prophet is a very powerful reality of the prophetic office. By now, we should be understanding and embracing more on how the full spectrum of the prophetic is not limited to the spoken word of prophecy. It is now obvious why the office of the prophet does not exist so that we can publicly show people how well we can prophesy.

The prophetic office exists so that those who operate under its mantle and the anointings associated with it can impact nations and generations. As we have learned, using Abraham as an example, the prophet's office is more powerful than the display of prophetic gifting, and there is a weight and authority that is being restored to this office. Prophets

Jonathan Ferguson

demonstrate their office in many ways and have multiple job descriptions that qualify them as the officers that they are. Over the next chapter, we will take the time and cover more of the basic foundations necessary in order to better understand this truth.

Chapter 3
Defining the Role of the Prophet

Chapter Objectives:
- Learn three basic things to consider when defining the role of the prophet
- Understand why it's important to study Hebraic definitions of the word "prophet"
- Learn the prophet's role as an officer
- Learn the prophet's role in shifting atmospheres, altering spiritual climates, and manifesting the supernatural
- Learn three dynamics of the "seer" in scripture
- Learn how the seer's anointing & the Issachar anointing connect
- Learn the prophet's role as a gatekeeper and guardian

Once we realize that the prophet's mantle and office extend far beyond the gift of prophecy, the common question becomes, "How do we discover what a prophet is and what he does?" The answer is that *there is no one answer* to this question.

Jonathan Ferguson

There are at least *three basic things* that we must consider in our process of researching who and what a prophet is. First, we must consider the Hebraic definitions of the word prophet found in the Old Testament. Next, we should consider the history of the prophets. Lastly, we have to consider the authority of prophet.

Three basic things to consider in defining the prophet's role:

1) Hebraic definitions
2) History of the Prophet
3) Authority of the Prophet

I am going take the next couple of chapters to explain these very three things previously listed. Each one represents a core understanding that I want to take a chapter for each to explain. This will help you begin to understand exactly what a prophet is and what he does.

In this chapter we will start by explaining the Hebraic definitions for the word prophet. And in doing so, we will define the role of the prophet. There are some things we just will not understand about the prophet until we understand from a Hebraic perspective what the Bible means when it mentions the prophet. To accomplish this, we must research the Hebraic definitions of the word "prophet" used in the Old Testament.

My Recommendation & Helpful Study References

Some may disagree about studying the Hebraic definitions for the word prophet from the Old Testament. The reason being is because many disagree concerning whether the New Testament prophets function as the Old Testament prophets did. However, despite the contradiction, New Testament prophets do not lack any capabilities of the Old Testament prophets. For more study on the how the New Testament prophet presently functions in the capacity of the Old Testament prophets and even greater, I strongly recommend that you register for my online school of the prophets at www.JCFNOW.com.

There are fifteen "ON DEMAND" videos that are available for a very small registration fee of only fifty dollars. You can learn more about the parallels of the Old and New Testament prophets at the school of the prophets; however, my assignment in this book is not to focus on that particular debate. You will find that the online school of the prophets is a great reference for relevant, wholesome, and revelatory teaching on the prophetic office.

Why Study Hebraic Definitions of the Prophet?

As I have mentioned, the first thing we need to do in order to define the role of the prophet is biblically define the word "prophet" from its original Hebraic roots in the Old Testament. It is important to do a word

Jonathan Ferguson

study on the prophet because the Hebraic language is more holistic than the Western. The English language, on the contrary, is often accustomed to categorizing key definitions very vaguely and narrowly.

It scares me when I hear a preacher say that he/she defined a biblical word from Webster's dictionary. Webster will not suffice because one English word can represent multiple Hebraic words, which all would have different definitions. Defining from Webster alone can leave us narrow minded and almost helplessly ignorant on any biblical subject. We must go deeper in our studies.

When we see the word prophet in the Bible, there are three different primary Hebraic words from which it can be translated. These three words are also foundational, having additional relative words that define what a prophet is as well. By merely defining the words, we learn that the role of the prophet is more extensive than we realized.

We learn the many job descriptions of the prophet as the Hebraic words are defined one by one. I actually began this process in my book entitled *Experiencing God in the Supernatural,* yet in this book I will cover more ground. However, I recommend both books to be studied because there are truths within *Experiencing God in the Supernatural* that I will not reiterate. You will find that this book goes more in depth as we deal with each Hebraic origin of the prophet. Now lets begin this journey with defining the word "Nabi."

NABI

The first and most prominent Hebraic word for the word prophet is Nabi, which means "to bubble up or boil over." It is also defined as "the inspired man" or "the official prophet," which in fact could be literally articulated by definition to be the office of the prophet. There are also a couple of relative Hebraic words such as "Nebuwauh" and "Nabyi," from which the working definition and explanation for Nabi is derived that I use in the following excerpt from my book *Experiencing God in the Supernatural*.

Excerpt:

The prophetic is an official administration within God's Kingdom. It is the "Nabi" function of the prophetic that distinguishes the prophet to serve as an ambassador with the full backing of Heaven's government. In fact, in Israel's ancient culture, the prophet would be equivalent to someone that had a high-ranking military position, or someone who was a governmental official. Furthermore, Nabi not only speaks of the office of the prophet, but also the inspiration of the prophet. The inspiration aspect of Nabi is the means by which a prophet is continually sensitive to discern the activities of the Spirit realm from which he serves and has citizenship, which is undoubtedly heaven. In fact, the fire in Jeremiah's bones was the stirring and bubbling of prophetic inspiration. It is a

Jonathan Ferguson

consistent stirring and awakening of the gifts inside that brings about a prophetic awareness and corresponding action in the lives of God's prophets. Both the inspiration and the office aspects of Nabi are intertwined. They cause the prophet to first discern the activity of heaven and next have the authority and power to initiate the alignment of the activities in earth with those of heaven—all through a spoken word.

It's important you understand why I expound upon "Nabi" the way that I do in the previous excerpt. The reason being is there are multiple factors we must take into consideration as we define "Nabi." When articulating a good working definition of "Nabi," we must examine multiple definitions of Hebraic words relative to "Nabi" and compare them with biblical examples.

I want to reiterate that one of the primary definitions for "Nabi" deals with inspiration, and the other deals with the authority of the office. When comparing the definitions to the life of Jeremiah, we understand that a prophet cannot exercise the authority to be the type of officer that "Nabi" defines him to be if he does not have great spiritual sensitivity. Furthermore, the prophet's spiritual sensitivity would only be to the measure of the "Nabi" boiling, burning, and bubbling inspiration within. Therefore, the office and the inspiration of the prophet work hand in hand.

We should also understand that every prophetic move is not a prophetic word, nor is it always predictive in nature. Sometimes when inspiration comes, there is a prophetic word; at other times, according to the previous excerpt, there is simply a "corresponding action" or what we can call a "prophetic gesture." These types of prophetic acts are powerful because they act out in the natural something symbolic of what's taking place in the Spirit world so that what is happening in the Spirit can manifest in the natural (Ezekiel 4:1-8; Isaiah 20:2-3).

Everything that the prophet is inspired and led of the Holy Ghost to do is initiating a chain reaction of events that establishes the will of God in the earth. The Nabi role of the prophet empowers him so that even if he does not prophesy, everything he thinks, says, does, and even his mere existence brings the heavens and the earth back into divine alignment.

Jesus said that if we receive a prophet in the name of a prophet, we would receive the prophet's reward (Matthew 10:41). The word "name" literally means authority and character. Therefore, Jesus is literally speaking of receiving an individual in the office of the prophet and not merely receiving a prophecy.

Many times it's not a prophetic word that we have trouble receiving, but rather the office of the prophet because we have yet to recognize all it represents. However, the prophetic office is so powerful that simply being in the presence of the prophet will cause supernatural things to begin to take place. We

Jonathan Ferguson

will better understand this as we examine our next Hebraic word "Nataph."

NATAPH

The second Hebraic word I want to deal with is Nataph, which means to "fall in drops or to open the heavens." Not only is Nataph used for the word "prophet," but it is also one of the prominent words used for the word "prophesy." In *Experiencing God in the Supernatural*, I write about how this function of the prophet is one of the factors that actually causes the word of the Lord to come to pass. In other words, the Nabi functions cause the prophet to discern what God is doing in the heavens. Next, as they act or speak based on what is discerned, the Nataph function is then activated in order to set the word of the Lord in motion. Be sure to study the following excerpt concerning Nataph.

Excerpt:

A prophet is one who uses words to open the heavens. Communities, cities, and even nations can be changed as they speak because atmospheres, climates, and environments must adjust to their words. The spirit and words of a prophet have the power to produce a prophetic presence. According to Deuteronomy 32:2, the words of Moses would "fall in drops" on the people like dew and rain as he spoke the word of the Lord. This is symbolic of Moses speaking under a prophetic anointing. The intensity of his words pierced the atmosphere for open heaven manifestations. In other words, the word of a prophet creates an atmosphere for what he says to come to pass. The same thing that occurred with Moses took place with Peter in Acts 10:44. Peter was preaching under a prophetic anointing when "while he was yet preaching," the Holy Ghost fell upon everyone that heard the word. The same is true throughout the ministry of Jesus, in that as He taught, power was present to heal the sick (Luke 5:17). Whenever Jesus taught the word, the atmosphere became conducive for miracles, signs, and wonders.

In addition to the previous excerpt, we should understand that Nataph deals with prophetic presence and atmosphere beyond that which is released through the spoken word. It's the very existence, aura, and persona of a prophet that can cause atmospheres to shift. The very presence of the prophet alone has the power to alter spiritual climates.

For example, in 2 Kings 4:8-11, Elisha did not tell the Shunammite woman that he was a prophet; however, there was something about his presence as he passed through her region that adjusted the spiritual climate. The same thing was felt in the city of Naioth in Ramah where Samuel the prophet dwelt. The spirit of prophecy would hover over the city and there was a felt prophetic presence even in the surrounding regions (1 Samuel 19:20-24).

The same should be true of prophets today. The weight of the prophet's mantle should be felt in his or her presence alone, and there are times in which a prophet should not have to say a word at all. One of the primary operations of the Nataph is to open the heavens in ways that divinely alters atmospheres, climates, and cultures so that miracles, signs, and wonders can be released. Therefore, once again we see the overall role of the prophet extending beyond verbal capacities through the prophet's Nataph abilities.

CHOZEH

The next Hebraic word is Chozeh, which means "seer, beholder in a vision, to contemplate with pleasure, to provide, and to see." There are three dynamics of what the seer represents in scripture that we should understand. One dynamic is the office of the seer, which is in actuality the office of the prophet, but more specifically, a position that a proficient prophet was given by a king. A seer is a prophet and a prophet is a seer, yet one who had been given the official position or title of a Seer had a specific responsibility as a prophet to be an advisor to the king.

The second dynamic is the "label" that was given to prophets by the people of Israel prior to Samuel re-establishing the office of the prophet in its fullness. We will explain these two dynamics of the seer more in this book when we deal with the origin of the school of the prophets along with various prophetic anointings and assignments in the next chapter. For now, I only want to introduce you to this dynamic and leave it alone until later.

The third dynamic of the seer is the nature of the seer's anointing. The grace of a seer is inclusive of prophetic abilities beyond the inspiration that comes with the Nabi function of the prophet. The seer's dimension of the prophet deals with both the ability to receive a message through inspiration and visual communication as opposed to inspiration only.

It's important when teaching concerning the seer to emphasize what particular dynamic we are dealing with in order to limit confusion. In addition to the three dynamics of the seer, there are also two other Hebraic words in particular that are important to define in order to help us understand the seer function of the prophet foundationally and more holistically. Those two words are "Roeh" and "Shamar." Let's take a moment to first review an excerpt concerning "Chozeh" and "Roeh." Afterwards, we will deal with a concept of "Shamar" that I did not include in the book *Experiencing God in the Supernatural*.

Excerpt:

Chozeh is the ability to see things in the Spirit and interpret the visions and images into a message. Prophets bring understanding, relevance, and can both accurately and plainly articulate spiritual things. This implies that the ability to see alone does not qualify the prophetic function of a "seer." Chozeh has a lot to do with the process of perception and interpretation concerning what is being seen. This ability is one that is developed over time, as a prophet is equipped in all the aspects of "seeing." He or she then becomes competent in processing what is seen for prophetic delivery. Therefore, we can't completely examine Chozeh without examining other aspects of what it means to see in the Spirit. There are many aspects of the seer's anointing, but I only want to cover the "Roeh" and "Shamar" aspects of what it means to be able to see in the Spirit in reference to the office of the prophet.

5. Roeh: to see

Psalm 23:1 The LORD is my shepherd; I shall not want.

The word Shepherd is descriptive of the pastoral anointing and derives from the original word "Roeh," which literally means, "to see". This aspect of spiritual vision deals with the release of progressive revelation, which causes prophets to know the divine counsel and instructions of God. It can also cause prophets to be born with a high inclination to creativity, which eventually causes them to become builders and trendsetters. For this reason, the ability to see in the prophetic and the pastoral anointing go hand in hand. Could it be that David and Moses experienced aspects of their prophetic preparation while tending to sheep? The shepherd's job is to be able to look ahead and steer the sheep in the proper direction. Prophets are needed to work very closely with pastors; at times, they also have the ability to pastor. They are well equipped to teach, impart, and train. This empowerment of spiritual vision enables prophets to disciple others because they not only master what they do, but they have the ability to train others to do the same. As they are looking ahead to see what direction the church should be going in, they are not only preparing people to move ahead, but they are also training others to maintain where the church has been. As this takes place, responsibilities are delegated normally through a type of ordination so that the church does not lose any ground gained as it moves on into its next dimension of effectiveness.

The prophet has a Shepherd's function of guidance and counseling to direct believers in the ways of the Lord. The history of the prophets shows that the Roeh function was often used to offer counsel to the kings of Israel as "Seers," which is symbolic of the apostolic and prophetic collaboration. Prophets have great wisdom and apostolic insight that equips them as Divine strategists in the Kingdom of God. Competent prophets have apostolic grace and are even at times chosen by the Lord for apostolic succession and ordination. This is why most of the prominent prophets of the Old Testament had ministries that closely resembled the apostolic ministry patterned in the New Testament. In fact, without apostolic and prophetic foundation, the pastoral anointing would have no basis of effectiveness (Ephesians 2:20).

SHAMAR

The last Hebraic word I would like to define is Shamar. Although it is not one of the three primary Hebraic words for the prophet, I reiterate that it is very important to define in order to better understand the

Jonathan Ferguson

function of Chozeh. The word Shamar means "watchman." And as a watchman, prophets are intercessors, warriors, and they are gatekeepers.

In *Experiencing God in the Supernatural*, I expound on the intercessory and warrior's function of the prophet. However, in this book, I believe we should get a better understanding of the prophet as a gatekeeper. In order to do so we must understand the gates that they are charged to keep.

Gates were scripturally represented as the places of counsel, decision-making, business transactions, and public influence. They are also immigration posts, security checkpoints, places of imports, and places of export. Simply put, as gatekeepers, prophets decide what's coming in and what's going out. They release prominence, they monitor influence, and they initiate divine exchanges.

In addition to scriptural representation of gates, there are many things of which gates are spiritually symbolic. And out of them all, timing is a very key gate in dealing with the prophet. I don't believe it is coincidence that the Jews divide the time of a day into eight compartments called "watches."

There are four watches of the day and four watches of the night, which is evidence that timing was key in the role of the watchman. I believe that this is proof that the Issachar anointing has its origin in the seer's anointing and function of the prophet. As a watchman, prophets are equipped with an incredible sense of time, causing them to always be able to discern the proper plan of action (Ecclesiastes 8:5; 1 Chronicles 12:32).

We will deal with this more in detail over the next chapter, but for now, Joseph is a great example of this truth. As a seer, he dreamed and interpreted the dreams of others, but by the Issachar anointing, he gave instructions that affected the next fourteen years of everyone on the face of the earth. Joseph functioned in a powerful capacity as a prophet in that he operated in both the Chozeh and Issachar functions of the prophet.

The life of Joseph is a key observation in understanding how to distinguish a more complete scope of prophetic activity. Just because an individual dreams prophetically does not mean that he or she is able to interpret dreams. Another individual may dream prophetically and interpret dreams also, but doesn't mean that he or she understands the times and the seasons. Likewise, I reiterate that just because an individual can prophesy, it does not make him a prophet. This is why it is very important that an individual is equipped as a prophet beyond the obvious and more surface-level operations of prophecy.

Jonathan Ferguson

The Prophet in Full Capacity

It is important we understand the expanded abilities and role of one who walks in the office of the prophet. However, after we have that understanding, it is also important to understand how those abilities are often clustered in the way prophets operate. Once we comprehend this, we understand why it is necessary for a prophet to understand his role holistically and be properly equipped to function therein.

We need prophets in this hour who function in full capacity. We also need those in the body of Christ who've graduated from being merely fascinated with a high-powered word of knowledge or gift of prophecy to begin placing a demand on the fullness of the prophet's mantle. This is why this chapter was written. It was written to begin a paradigm shift in your thinking that will cause you to crave the true expression of the prophetic.

I believe this chapter has been *that paradigm shift* for many of you, but as we conclude this chapter I want to make sure you don't just move on with a lot of information. I want you to be sure you have a broader concept concerning the role of the prophet. So, let's make sure we pull together everything we have covered so far. And as we do, we will be better prepared to continue examining the full capacity of the prophet in more detail throughout the next chapter.

Prophets: 101

Conclusion

As we now see, there are many things we can learn about the prophet by just doing a word study. In doing so we discover that the role of the prophet is by far more expanded than what is assumed of most. And we finally embrace the fact that a prophet is one who does more than prophesy.

We also understand that in order to fulfill the role of a prophet, an individual would need great spiritual sensitivity. And even more so than an inward witness, the sensitivity should include an ability to see into various depths of the Spirit. They would need this in order to be able to exercise spiritual authority in ways that brings the heavens and earth into divine alignment.

We have learned that a prophet's prophetic presence is to be felt beyond the words he speaks. That the weight of the mantle has the power to shift atmospheres, adjust spiritual climates, and alter cultures. We also see now that prophets operate under open heavens in order to invoke the supernatural, and they are gatekeepers over spiritual territories.

This means that they govern over regions and spiritually monitor them. They either approve or disapprove what gets in and what goes out. They are warriors who guard what is entrusted to the people of God, and intercession is something they live. And they are kingdom analysts and strategists always equipped

Jonathan Ferguson

to offer wise council necessary for both preservation and forward advancement.

It should now be clear to you that there are many anointings and abilities that are in operation when dealing with the office of the prophet that often go overlooked. The role of the prophet is obviously inclusive of more than being a mouthpiece or a spokesman. A prophet is without doubt called to do more than merely say what God is saying.

When dealing with the prophetic in times past we have over emphasized the prophetic word, but have had no idea the behind the scenes job description of the prophet. In fact, it is the work that prophets accomplish in the realm of the Spirit that is more prominent than any of their activity in the public will ever be. This is why they have to know their backing power and authority in the supernatural and be mature and trustworthy enough to carry such a weight in the Kingdom of God.

Now that this foundation is laid, we can explore some key elements concerning the history of the prophets in the next chapter that will help us understand various prophetic anointings and assignments necessary to the prophetic mantle. Trust me, it only gets more interesting as we progress in understanding more holistically who and what prophets are and what they are called to do.

Chapter 4
History of the Prophets

Chapter Objectives:
- Review the primary functions of various historical prophets
- Learn why the School of the Prophets was established
- Learn what basic prophetic abilities and anointing come under the prophet's schooling
- Learn why prayer and evangelism are unavoidable fundamentals in the life of the prophet
- Learn what it means for a prophet to function in full capacity

Your history homework

In addition to defining the role of the prophet from its Hebraic roots, another thing that will help us discover who prophets are and what they are called to do would be to understand their history. As we examine historically, we understand more how the qualifications and abilities that accompany the prophet's mantle are exhaustive. We also see how each successive prophet had an assignment and role relevant to the particular culture they lived in at the time.

For example, Samuel was more of a priestly prophet while Daniel was more of a governmental prophet. In fact, even the nature of certain prophets' temperament was prophetic of their calling and purpose. For example, Isaiah is known historically as more of an eagle eye prophet while Jeremiah is remembered as the weeping prophet. Elijah was known as more of an abrasive type while Moses was commended of God in being the meekest and most humble man on the face of the earth during his lifetime.

A man of God once told me to search the Bible and find everything that God said about every particular prophet in order to understand what a prophet is. This is helpful because there is a conglomerate of the prophetic office's key components patterned historically in scripture. This means that we can examine and combine the successive anointings of historical prophets in order to further clarify the prophet's job description.

I'm not going to do this in this book, but it will make great homework for you as the reader and it will require patience to complete. My job in this chapter is rather to lay a different foundation concerning the prophetic timeline. The particular area of prophetic history that I want to examine in this chapter is the history of the school of the prophets. As we do so, there are truths that have been hidden concerning the office of the prophetic that we will begin to understand in a greater measure.

Restoring Prophetic Fundamentals:

Before we explore anything about the prophetic schools, we should understand that out of everything that they represent, there are two things that a modern day school of the prophets must restore back at the foundation of teaching. Those two things are both *prayer* and *evangelism*. One of the first things that should take place in the life of one who is called as a prophet is an increased desire to pray. The next is that they should have a desire that everyone come to know Jesus.

The testimony of Jesus is the spirit of prophecy. In other words, prophecy is ultimately about Jesus and what He did to redeem mankind and should never represent anything less. When we abandon the spirit of prophecy, we will get it wrong all the time. I know this part of the book completely shifts the tone of my writing, but this is exactly where the Holy Ghost wanted me to write this because He now has your attention.

It does not matter how deep and profound we become in our understanding and practice of the prophetic if we lose the fundamentals of prayer and evangelism. Have you answered the call to prayer? Have you answered the call to see souls saved? If not, you have not answered the call of the prophet.

Do you understand the importance and urgency of prayer? Do you understand the importance and urgency of the lost coming to know Jesus? If not, you don't understand the prophetic.

Being prophetic is about being so close to Jesus that it becomes normal to know His voice. Being prophetic is about being so full of the Spirit that testifies of Jesus (John 15:26) that you become consumed with a desire that everyone comes to know Jesus (Acts 1:8). A prophetic school should never prize learning to prophesy and learning about the prophetic above learning to pray and effectively learning to share Jesus with those who are not saved.

I believe that when these priorities are not in place, two immediate things will take place. One, it will only slow down the student's progress and growth in the prophetic. Two, it will leave room for an individual's motive of operating in the prophetic to become tainted and perverted.

I believe that when we return to the spirit of prophecy, not only will we prophesy more accurately, but also Jesus will be sure that we are fully equipped as prophets in ways beyond prophecy to effectively testify of and represent who He is. Everything we are learning about the prophetic means nothing without prayer and evangelism becoming two of the primary calls to action concerning the role of the prophet. My recommendation is that you understand this before you attempt to understand anything else about the prophetic.

Why the School of the prophets Originated

1 Samuel 9:9 records that in the days prior to Samuel, prophets were known as seers; however, scriptures are also very clear that in the days of Moses, prophets were recognized as prophets and not seers. It is important we have clarity concerning what took place in the space of time between the days of Moses until the days of Samuel.

1 Samuel 3:1, 19-21 gives us that clarity as it says that the word of the Lord was rare. In other words, there are times in which the prophetic is not as prevalent as in other times. And I believe this is why men begin to recognize prophets as seers and not prophets, which is very significant. Let me explain.

The word seer in 1 Samuel 9:9 is *not* translated from the Hebraic word *Chozeh*, which is one of the primary words for the word prophet in the scripture as we have explained in the previous chapter. The revelation of 1 Samuel 9:9 is that the people only recognized the prophet by one dimension of his anointing. Their comprehension of who the prophet is was based on very limited knowledge. This is significant because it is very similar to how the prophetic office is being treated today.

I believe that God raised up Samuel to reinstitute the office of the prophet in its fullness and redefine what a prophet is. This means that when Samuel established the school of the prophets, it began a process of restoring holistic prophetic ministry in the earth. And it is time we also raise the standard of prophetic expression and return to the biblical concepts of what God originally intended for the prophet to represent.

We see clearly in 1 Samuel 9:9 that the people historically began to recognize prophets by their ability to see in the spirit, although we clearly understand that being a prophet is inclusive of more than that. I believe that it was only after Samuel reinstituted the office of the prophet and established the school that the people's understanding of the prophetic began to change. Although prophets occasionally would continue to be recognized as seers, the concept of what a seer was had evolved.

Israel had begun to make great progress in understanding the prophetic after Samuel. Therefore, the seer had eventually begun to represent more than what it did in 1 Samuel 9:9 after the school of the prophets came about. The seer had gradually begun to represent a prophet with governmental placement along with diplomatic rights and privileges. In order to understand this, take time to review the following expert from a book I wrote entitled *Learning the Language of God*.

EXCERPT from *Learning the Language*:

Historically, a Seer is more than someone with an ability to see in the Spirit. A seer is what a prophet was referred to as prior to Samuel establishing the kingdom of Israel, and fully re-instituting the office of the prophet (1 Samuel 9:9). From the time of Samuel and throughout the reign of Israel's kingdom, the title of "seer" and "prophet" were used interchangeably, although it was customary for prophets who worked closely with kings to be known as seers (2 Samuel 24:11; 1 Chronicles 29:29).

Scripturally, a seer had a governmental office in Israel's culture. They were advisors to the king responsible to give detailed and specific counsel concerning the forward progress of the nation and one could not fill this office with mere prophetic ability. A seer was not just any prophet, but a very proficient prophet that worked for the government. In fact, the title of seer is more of a secular title for a prophet with a position of governmental influence. Historically, a prophet could not hold such a position apart from a certain measure of prophetic scholastics. Their level of proficiency as prophets also caused them to be esteemed among the company of prophets as either fathers or masters (2 Kings 2:3, 12), and they were known for their ability to train others to walk in the prophetic anointing. Modern day seers would be well-equipped individuals who walk in the office of the prophet and yet hold influential positions of leadership in the secular world.

Jonathan Ferguson

Review of Three Dynamics of the Seer

There is without question a historical understanding of seers being proficient prophets. However, we must understand that until the school of prophets was established, to be a seer only represented one dimension of the prophetic anointing. It wasn't until after Samuel that seers represented more than those who only walked in a specific dimension of the prophetic anointing. Let's take a moment to review the three dynamics of what the seer scripturally represented.

Remember, one dynamic of the seer is the nature of the seer's anointing, which is inclusive of prophetic abilities beyond the inspiration that is associated with the Nabi function of the prophet. Another dynamic is the office of the seer, which is in actuality is the office of the prophet, but more specifically, a position that a proficient prophet was given by a king. If you have not read the previous excerpt from *Learning the Language of God*, be sure to go back and review it in order to understand this truth.

The last dynamic of the seer and one that is most relative to this chapter is in reference to how in 1 Samuel 9:9, the term "Seer" was originally a title that was given to prophets by people who did not understand the prophetic holistically. In fact, during the era of 1 Samuel 9:9, what the people of Israel understood the seer to be was completely different than what the kings recognized the seers to be in the times afterward.

Prophets: 101

1 Samuel 9:9 represents a unique era for the prophet unlike any other time in history. It was a transitional time in which the prophetic ministry was being redefined. This is why the establishing of the school of the prophets was a very significant reformation of the prophetic in which Samuel played a key role.

If it were not for Samuel establishing the school of the prophets, the prophetic would have continued to be recognized by only one dimension of its anointing possibly for centuries to come. The school of the prophets was and is therefore very necessary to be established in order that the full expression and nature of the prophet will emerge and be understood. Now that we understand the history of why the school was necessary, let's examine some more basics concerning the school of the prophets and how it functions.

School of the Prophets and its Leadership

The school of the prophets was and is a company of prophetic people (1 Samuel 19:20-24; 2 Kings 2:3). It operated as a type of headquarters for prophetic ministry and exists so that senior prophets not only to train those who are called as prophets (Ephesians 4:11-12), but also to either train prophetic people in their particular prophetic anointings or simply help individuals discover their spiritual gifts (1 Timothy 4:14).

The heads of the school were often acknowledged as masters (2 Kings 2:3,5,16) and fathers (2

Jonathan Ferguson

Kings 2:12). However, to be identified as such in the prophetic was *not* an honorary title that was given. The objective was not for the senior leaders of the school to acquire a superior title such as "master prophet," but rather to acknowledge both the nature and proficiency of senior prophets.

    I reiterate, when we see prophets referenced in scripture as fathers and masters, we should not think "titles," but rather nature and proficiency. What do I mean by this? The nature of the senior prophet was that of a father and those under their tutelage were often referred to as sons (2 Kings 2:3).

    As fathers, the ultimate success of a prophet is not in the ability to maintain an influential and politically religious position in society, but rather to seek out and successfully train up successors. Therefore, the proficiency of the senior prophet would need to be that of a master. Just like with any other master's degree, it meant that they had acquired a certain amount of "credit hours" in experience. When someone reaches a level of mastery, it means that they are able to both do what they do very well and teach others to do it just as well or even better.

    Most importantly, even above their proficiency, senior prophets were validated according to their maturity in character (Matthew 7:15-20). From the times of Moses up until the times of Jesus, the criteria of the prophet had evolved beyond merely being prophetically accurate. And as we span the history of the prophets, we learn that it was their proficiency, experience, and reputation that positioned prophets as credible leaders.

Therefore, prophets were apt to confirm successive ministry leaders and release the impartation necessary for individuals to progress in the prophetic gifting. One could only rightly assume that this type of environment only re-enforced healthy and strong accountability. And in this type of environment, it would only be safe to believe that even if the prophetic gifting of one individual seemed to surpass that of a senior leader, the pupils were yet able to discern the difference between gifting and office, and ultimately stay in their lane.

Schooling Multiple Prophetic Anointings

In addition to imparting prophetic anointing and training prophetic successors, the school of the prophets existed to monitor spiritual activity and acclimate people to the supernatural. This is a very important factor for us to understand because of the demonic world's counterpart for the prophetic. When the scriptures mention the counterpart of the prophetic, there are multiple factors included.

In fact, Deuteronomy 18:10-12 mentions eight different avenues from which the demonic counterpart of the prophetic operates. We would be mistaken

Jonathan Ferguson

to believe that the counterpart of the prophetic functioned in more capacity than the prophetic itself. Furthermore, it would be silly to believe that a witch would be more versatile in spiritual abilities than a prophet is.

    We should be able to see clearly now that when God calls an individual into the office of the prophet, there are multiple abilities and gifting that come under their schooling. It is for this reason that prophets should be well prepared in order to ensure they are ready to utilize all that God has packed in their arsenals.

    When a prophet is operating in full capacity, it is like a safe guard that prevents individuals from ever needing to be curious of exploring its counterparts. The following is an extremely brief and basic synopsis of the gifting and abilities that are represented in a typical school of the prophets. It is by far not an exhaustive list; however, it will continue to help us embrace the biblical concept of the prophet's spiritual diversity.

Typical prophetic types among the school of prophets:

    Seers (2 Kings 17:13)
    Dreamers (Deuteronomy 13:1-5)
    Interpreters (Daniel 1:17; Daniel 5:12)
    Intercessors (Jeremiah 27:18; Ezekiel 13:4-5)
    Scribes — prophetic writers (Jeremiah 36:26-28)

Minstrels — prophetic musicians (2 Kings 3:15)
Psalmist — prophetic singers and songwriters (2 Samuel 23:1)

The previous chart pertaining to the school of the prophets only confirms what we have been learning concerning the host of prophetic abilities that expand beyond prophecy. The school of the prophets is significant in that it gives expression to and facilitates multiple prophetic anointings that entail the prophetic mantle in is fullness. In fact, these anointings are like subunits of the prophetic mantle.

They are very necessary to authentic and holistic prophetic expression. And as long as the school of the prophets was in place, it was less likely that the office of the prophet was validated on the basis of isolated prophetic capabilities. It is more likely that prophets understood the extent of their calling and received adequate schooling and experience to successfully operate therein.

The Prophet Full in Capacity

As I have previously mentioned, if we look at the prophets historically, we see that every prophet had a primary anointing that they functioned in depending on their assignment. However, there is more that we can understand from the example of many historical prophets. If we combine the truths we have covered so far in this chapter and the previous chapter there are a few invaluable truths we have discovered.

One is that a prophet should be functioning at least within the capacity of what a prophet is by definition of the Hebraic origins of the word "prophet". Secondly, a prophet should also be aware of and be active in the basic anointings that come under their schooling. Lastly, a prophet has multiple prophetic abilities that he or she should be aware of and fully equipped to function in.

When studying the history of the prophets, understanding the uniqueness of each historical prophet is not enough. We should also understand that there are multiple qualities of a prophet that should be evident in every prophet regardless their individual uniqueness. We touched on this truth in the last chapter as we began to deal with the anointing of Issachar and its connection to the Hebraic words *Shamar* and *Chozeh*. I believe at this point we should revisit our study on the anointing of Issachar in order to further verify how multiple anointings are clustered in operation when the prophetic mantle is active in the life of a prophet.

The Prophetic Lineage of Issachar

Cross-referencing the anointing of Issachar in the lives of biblical prophets is a great illustration because of how the Issachar anointing is known as a historical prophetic anointing. We will see how this anointing

Prophets: 101

not only operated in the sons of Issachar, but also in the lives of many other prophets. It is as we examine how the anointing of Issachar is evident in the lives of prophets who are historically known for various and unique assignments that we will discover how different prophetic anointings are often clustered. We will use this as a pattern in further understanding that the prophet has multiple prophetic functions in which he is fully equipped and capable of operating in simultaneously.

The anointing of Issachar is that which discerns the times and seasons and has a divine knowing of what needs to be done in those times. Daniel is known for having a governmental anointing, yet it is the Issachar anointing on his life that is rarely acknowledged by many pertaining to being key in his success as a prophet. It was Daniel that read the prophecy of Jeremiah and understood that it was "time" for the prophecy to come to pass after the seventy years that had been predicted were fulfilled (Daniel 9).

Ezekiel also functions in this anointing as he prophetically declares in Ezekiel 12:25 that there would be no more delays. Isaiah operates in this same anointing in Isaiah 66:8. Therein, he declares the ability of God to cause a nation to be born at once and also causes the earth to bring forth a harvest in just one day. Even Jesus Himself operates in this anointing in Luke 4:17-19 as He stands to declare the acceptable time. He was in fact announcing Himself to be the "Lord of the

Jonathan Ferguson

release" and the one who prophetically initiates the year of jubilee.

Elisha also walks uniquely in this Issachar anointing in 2 Kings 4 and 7. In fact, in 2 Kings 4:16, Elijah prophesies the same words that God speaks to Abraham about Sarah giving birth (Genesis 18:10-14). Let me make it plain.

According to Genesis 18:10-14, Elijah was not the first to prophetically declare in 2 Kings 4:16, "about *this season* according to the time of life." This statement literally means "by this time next year," and it is without doubt an anointing to discern the time. Could it be that the Issachar anointing actually originated with Abraham? It would make sense because of how Issachar was in Abraham's loins just as Levi was when he tithed to Melchisedec (Hebrews 7:9-10).

Lets not forget that when "by this time next year" is mentioned to Abraham, the question is also asked " is there anything too hard for the Lord?" The question, by the way, was the same question stated to Jeremiah (Jeremiah 32:27; Genesis 18:14). No wonder Zechariah the prophet had the revelation that it is not by might nor by power but by the spirit of the Lord (Zechariah 4:6). In other words, it is the timing of God that aligns us with the ability of God. Prophets, make sure we are in the timing of God so that we are not doing things in our own strength.

The significance of studying Issachar

The previous examples are significant in a couple of ways. For one, they show how the prophets of old were not merely prophetic types who demonstrated only a distinct measure of the prophetic. Neither were they relegated to only operate in the anointing most relative to the nature of their assignment. This means that the biblical accounts of the prophets do not necessarily represent different types of prophetic callings for different types of prophets. However, they represent prophets who, although their assignments were specific, were yet operating in multiple prophetic anointings. They reveal how prophets actually function in a cluster of prophetic abilities and not just those that were more historically evident of their assignment.

Secondly, they are significant especially in how the anointing on the sons of Issachar trace back to Abraham. This means that every prophet not only has his or her own anointing and assignment, but also has a grace to walk in the successive anointings of the previous prophet that were essential to the prophetic mantle. In other words, the reality of how Daniel moved in the anointing of Issachar is no different in the way that Elisha moved in a double portion of Elijah's anointing. Even when John the Baptist came, he came in the spirit and power of Elijah.

Jonathan Ferguson

Conclusion

When beginning to understand more holistically what a prophet is and what they are called to do, there are a couple of more things that we have brought into consideration within this chapter. First, we have discovered that there is a conglomerate of the prophetic office's key components patterned historically in scripture. Although we did not go into detail about them, we understand that we should research this fact in order to further clarify the prophet's job description.

Secondly, as we examined the school of the prophets, we understood that there are some basic abilities that come under the prophet's schooling. Lastly, we understand that the anointings patterned historically in scripture, the abilities that come under a prophet's schooling, and the functionality of the prophet according it's Hebraic roots are all often clustered together in the way that a prophet operates in their mantle. If we began to practice referencing the previous in context of the prophet's holistic operations and responsibilities, we would find ourselves advancing tremendously in our understanding of authentic prophetic ministry.

I know that the concept may seem rather intimidating to consider in comparison to what we have typically been taught concerning the prophet's office, but it is not. As exhaustive as the description may appear, prophets should at least be aware of the anointings that correlate to the prophet's office throughout history. Furthermore, there should be no reason that a prophet does not at least function in the capacity of that which is in direct relation to the Hebraic definitions of the prophet.

I encourage every reader to often go back and study the Hebraic definitions of the prophet and attempt to track those anointings in the lives of the prophets throughout scripture. Likewise, we who are called to the prophetic should be wiling to examine ourselves in our calling and be sure that we biblically measure up to what it entails. There are only two options for those of us who claim the office of the prophet and yet do not manifest the expression that it truly represents. Either we need to reevaluate our calls or we need to be willing to go back to prophets 101 where class is always in session.

Chapter 5
The Authority of the Prophet

Chapter Objectives:
- Learn what distinguishes the authority of the prophet
- Learn four things that distinguish the words of a prophet
- Learn how the content of prophecy centers around a prophet's jurisdictional authority
- Learn how prophets expand and broaden the scope and measure of their authority

The last of three basic factors that we should examine in understanding what a prophet is and what they do is the authority of the prophet. The authority assigned to the office of the prophet is one of the main factors that distinguishes a prophet from a prophesier. In fact, there are a couple of things that distinguish the authority of a prophet.

The first thing that distinguishes the authority of the prophet that I would like to deal with is the prophet's jurisdiction. When dealing with a prophet's jurisdiction, we are dealing with the place of their assignment. This is very important because if you are a prophet, your primary prophetic anointing will be determined by the nature of your assignment, yet your prophetic authority will be determined by the place of assignment.

Every prophet has a jurisdiction. Some prophets are called to nations while other prophets are local. The prophet Jeremiah was called to nations yet the prophetess Anna only ministered in the temple continually (Jeremiah 1:5; Luke 2:36). For example, an individual can be called as a prophet in Tennessee and yet have no jurisdiction in California. This is called a measure of rule and the scriptures speak of such in 2 Corinthians 10:13-15.

Another thing that distinguishes the authority of the prophet is the angelic guard. However, the thing that distinguishes a prophet's authority most is not the angels, but the fact that they stand in God's presence (1 Kings 17:1). In the realm of the spirit, the highest position of authority is the right hand of power (Hebrews 1:13). The revelation is that God entrusts spiritual authority to individuals who are close to Him and spend time with Him. If Gabriel the angel was given great authority because of his position in the presence of God, how much more can individual who is made in God's image and likeness or one called to the office of the prophet (Luke 1:19)?

Prophets: 101

Lastly, prophets also have added weight and authority on the words that they speak. Moses and Aaron are great examples of this truth. God told Moses that when he spoke to Pharaoh, he would be as a god to him and yet Aaron would be as a prophet of Moses (Exodus 7:1). Even though both Moses and Aaron were speaking the same message to Pharaoh, the weight of their authority in the spirit realm was different.

This is important to distinguish because many have the Miriam and Aaron syndrome of "I can prophesy too" (Numbers 12:1-8). Even though not only Aaron, but also Miriam was a prophet, God made a distinction between when Moses spoke and when Miriam and Aaron prophesied. If this distinction is made among those who are called to the office of the prophet, how much more should the gift of prophecy also be properly ranked in comparison to the words of a prophet?

Just because a person prophesies doesn't mean that the particular prophecy has the authority or weight to move anything. We must discern this. For example, when an individual is prophesying as one who has the gift of prophecy, the results are that the recipient is built up, motivated, and strengthened (1 Corinthians 14:3). However, when an individual is prophesying as one who occupies the office of the prophet, there is an added authority in their words to accomplish a lot more than what the gift accomplishes. The following consists of a few things that distinguish the weight of the words spoken by one who occupies the office of the prophet.

The words of prophets:

A) Their Words come to pass
B) Their Words can initiate transformation
C) Their Words alter things: they create a chain reaction of events that bring about manifestation of spoken word
D) Their Words are signified and confirmed by signs and wonders

Jurisdictional Authority

One thing that we will notice concerning the authority of a prophet is that their prophecies will often center on their jurisdiction and assignment. No matter how accurate our prophetic gifting is we will find that in our prophetic ministries, God will rarely speak to us outside of our jurisdiction. Therefore, you can always measure the weight and authority of prophets by the scope of their prophecy. This is in fact the difference between someone who is prophesying houses and cars versus someone who is prophesying to the government. There comes a time when governments need prophets whom God has given jurisdiction to arise and begin to deal with the weightier matters of a nation.

Abraham had so much authority in God, as we have previously examined in chapter two, that God had given him jurisdiction in Sodom and Gomorrah even though he was not physically located in those regions. Even Ezekiel at times would be shown things that were taking place in Israel while he was located among the captives at Babylon. One way we know if we are called to the nations as prophets is by what extent our jurisdiction expands beyond our geographical location. Moses is another great example of this in that he received the revelation and assignment for Egypt while he was yet in Midian. When crises take a nation by surprise, it's often because prophets are out of their jurisdictions.

How a Prophet Broadens their Scope of Authority

The greatest way to broaden the scope and measure of our jurisdictional authority as prophets is to broaden our intercession. There are so many prophetic anointings buried inside of people because they would rather have a title than have a prayer life. The proof that God was able to trust Abraham with the type of jurisdictional authority given to him was seen when he humbled himself in prayer for Sodom. Intercession is the birthing canal of the prophetic. This is one reason why when the scripture first mentions Abraham as a prophet, it was in the context of God commending Abraham's prayer life to the King Abimelech (Genesis 20:3-7).

Another way that God broadens the prophet's authority is through humility. In fact, one of the main

Jonathan Ferguson

agendas that God has assigned in prayer is that of humbling ourselves (James 4:6-8). Even with Moses, as God distinguished the weight of his words versus the prophecies of Miriam and Aaron, it was his meekness that was commended.

Likewise, Elisha's humility is commended in scripture in that he was known as one that washed the hands of Elijah. In other words, it was Elisha's humility in serving Elijah that was key concerning his transition into the office of the prophet. Prophets have to know the order of the centurion, which is the ability to understand that to be in authority is to be under authority (Matthew 8:8-9).

It is very important that if we are going to expand our authority as prophets, we must learn to both humble ourselves and pray. Elijah had great authority in his words to even control weather patterns just by praying and standing in the presence of God. Sad thing is that many prophets today would rather have a title than have real power with God.

Added Authority

Another amazing truth concerning the authority of the prophet is that there are prophets who are given by God dual "doma" gifts. What do I mean by this? When the scriptures speak of the five-fold ministry gifts, the word gift is translated from the word "doma" (Ephesians 4:8-12). To have a dual "doma" gift would mean that an individual is called to more than one five-fold ministry office. Paul is a great example of this when the scripture mentions how he is called by God as a teacher, evangelist, and apostle (2 Timothy 1:11).

It is very possible to have a dual "doma" calling. In fact, there are some prophets that are called to both the apostolic and prophetic office. This dual "doma" cluster enables the prophet to function in an added authority within his prophetic office, especially when the apostolic begins to awaken in them. This is very possible because of how the apostolic and prophetic can often function as partnering mantles according to Ephesians 2:20. In fact, the prophets in the book of Acts were known for playing key roles in apostolic ministry (Acts 13:1; Acts 21:8-12).

There is often a closer parallel among the apostles and prophets than we realize. I believe this is why the ministries of many prominent Old Testament prophets resemble the ministries of the New Testament apostles. It should not seem absurd for a spiritually minded individual to embrace the reality of how prophets can assume an added weight of authority on their mantles because of their calling to the apostolic. This is likely one of the reasons that Jesus said of John that He was more than a prophet (Matthew 11:9-11).

I have even witnessed by observation how some of the powerful apostles of today first acknowledged

Jonathan Ferguson

and accepted the call of the prophet in their lives. The point is that authority and influence can evolve for the prophets who are committed to humbling themselves in seeking the Lord. When we truly begin maximizing our calling, the scriptures teach that if we are faithful over few, we will be made rulers over much.

Conclusion

When we consider the Hebraic definitions of a prophet, the history of the prophets, and the authority of the prophet, there is much that can be learned about the prophetic office. As a result, it becomes easier to recognize the difference between someone who only operates in the gift of prophecy and someone who operates in the mantle of the prophet. And now that these basics are covered, we can begin to explore throughout the remaining chapters certain truths that have been hidden for ages concerning the impact of authentic prophets.

There are powerful truths concerning the prophetic that have been lost due to how many neglect the ministry of the prophet. And there are many that neglect the ministry of the prophet because of how little it is mentioned in the New Testament. As a result, the office of the pastor is most embraced in the modern day church although it is the least mentioned office in New Testament scriptures. In fact, the ratio of how much more the New Testament mentions the office of the prophet in comparison to the office of the pastor is well beyond one hundred references versus the one time that the office of the pastor is mentioned.

Am I implying that the office of the prophet is more important the office of the pastor? Of course not! Don't get ahead of me. Just keep reading. You will understand in a moment.

What many don't understand about why prophets are not mentioned as often in the New Testament is that the early believers already had a healthy paradigm concerning the prophet. There was no reason to reintroduce the office of the prophet in the New Testament writings. However, there was a need to spend more time introducing the office of the apostle. And it is the office of the apostle that the New Testament focuses its attention on.

Although this book is not about the apostle, there is one key revelation we should understand concerning the apostolic prior to moving forward in our studies. The revelation is that in our present day there must be yet another shift in the prophetic if there is to be a complete restoration of the apostolic. In fact, it is the lack of this particular paradigm shift that I believe is the reason why although the apostle is the most mentioned office in the New Testament, it is yet still the most misunderstood. It is for this same reason that the prophetic is most resisted although the pastoral is the most embraced.

Jonathan Ferguson

You have to hear me in the Spirit in this matter. Let me make it clear. I am not saying at all that any five-fold ministry office should be embraced more than the other. I'm rather saying that according to New Testament pattern of ministry, there is no reason that every five-fold ministry office should not be embraced as much as the pastor is. And this is very key in understanding the necessity of embracing the prophetic office in a way that both the prophetic and apostolic ultimately have the type of platform needed to facilitate the last and greatest- Book of Acts type of awakening and move of God that is on the horizon.

It is only after the prophetic is in full capacity that the stage is set for the apostles to fully emerge. Many have believed that the prophetic and the apostolic have been completely restored, but there is yet another shifting. In fact, the reason you are reading this book now is because there is another shift coming to the prophetic movement. Now let's go deeper in our understanding of the prophetic, and in doing so, prepare for the shift that is ahead.

Chapter 6
The Shift

Chapter Objectives:
- Understand historically how the life of Samuel correlates with the current shift in the prophetic
- Embrace a shift in the maturity and integrity of the prophetic
- Understand why it is important to begin understanding the prophetic from a Kingdom perspective

The life of Samuel is very key in how the prophetic anointing began to shift historically. Samuel was an important prophet in that he both anointed the first two kings of Israel and established the office of the prophet as an official institution within Israel's culture. In fact, I believe that it is interesting how the establishing of the school of the prophets was during the same time in which Samuel the prophet anointed the first two king of Israel.

I also believe that there are a few dynamics within the historical account of the two kingly anointings that can be paralleled to how the prophetic anointing is shifting. Therefore, I would like to briefly examine the original two kingly anointings as illustrations of how I believe the prophetic anointing is now shifting out of one place into the place where it operates how God originally ordained it.

In order to help paint the picture, let's propose that the anointings of Saul and David represent two different waves, eras, or movements of the prophetic. Long story short, it was Saul that was anointed first and David that was anointed second (1 Sam 10:1; 1 Sam 16:13). Furthermore, Saul was the people's choice and David was God's choice.

Likewise, I believe that the first wave of the prophetic was what the people wanted, but the second is shifting the prophetic back to what God wanted. In other words, the prophetic has become a lot of things that it does not biblically represent, but God is releasing another movement of the prophetic in the earth in which we will see prophets that arise and do the will of the Father.

For example, one of the things that have stood out in the first wave of the prophetic movement is the accuracy of the prophetic word. However, I believe that the body of Christ is beginning to realize that although prophets should prophesy accurately there is more that their mantles have to offer. Let me explain.

Prophets: 101

The bible speaks of how prophecy is a sign. The purpose of signs and wonders is to verify the power of God in ways that draw people to Jesus. This is why the accuracy of the prophetic is important. It verifies that Jesus is speaking through an individual and causes people to know that the prophetic is real. However, there are yet other dimensions of the prophetic needed to be active in the life of the prophet.

When prophets do not understand the fullness of their calling, it becomes easier for them to allow the people to pressure them into functioning like a psychic. This has become a huge misrepresentation of the prophetic throughout the body of Christ. For example, the first thing that most people do when they find out that an individual is a prophet is ask for "a word," not understanding that although a prophet can prophesy, there are times in which God does not allow them to (Micah 2:6; 2 Peter 1:21).

In fact, many prophets begin by attempting to perform in the way that the people prefer instead of functioning in the specific prophetic capacity that is relevant in executing their God-given task. When this happens their growth is stunted and their gifts are prostituted. Ministry for them becomes about who can prophesy the best, who can raise the most money, and whose itinerary is full instead of who is fulfilling the prophetic assignment on their lives. Better yet who is even acclimated to the abilities that God has equipped

Jonathan Ferguson

the prophet with in order to fulfill their prophetic assignment.

THAT DAY IS OVER. The prophetic is shifting. God didn't design the prophetic to fulfill the desires of the people, but rather to communicate His heart to His people. There is a new era of the prophetic anointing that is emerging. There is a company of prophetic people that will return to the fullness of what the prophetic biblically represents.

Back to Saul and David

There are a couple of more things I believe we should understand about the anointing of David and Saul and how it correlates to the present shift in the prophetic movement. When Samuel anointed Saul, he anointed him with a vial of oil (1 Samuel 10:1). This is significant in that when judgments are poured from heaven in the book of Revelations, they are poured out from a vial.

God was obviously not pleased with the people's choice of leadership. It was almost as if God was saying, "Although I'm going to allow you to be promoted it will not excuse you from the consequences of your rebellion." Likewise, I believe there are some prophets who are represented now in this first wave of the prophetic restoration who are in some serious trouble if they do not repent.

However, when Samuel anointed David, he did not anoint him with a vial. David was God's choice, and when the prophet was sent to anoint him, he was sent to anoint him with a horn of oil (1 Samuel 16:13). The horn is significant all throughout scripture because it symbolizes exalted authority and dominion. There's a dimension of authority in the prophetic office that the kingdom has yet to see because there have been too many individuals satisfied with playing around in prophetic kindergarten. Thank God that this is changing and the prophetic movement is beginning to mature and understand its true calling.

Purifying Current Prophetic Models

We should understand that God's first agenda through Samuel was modeling the prophetic in a way to prepare Israel for the kingdom (1 Samuel 9:22; 1 Samuel 10:5, 10-11). However, the people of Israel were trying to birth the kingdom before its time and they were missing a key element, which is the prophetic (1 Samuel 12:1-25). God ordained that the people have a king, but when they wanted a king, it was not yet time for a king. As we follow the timeline, we see that God eventually sent Samuel to anoint Saul to be king, but he was anointed with that which represented judgment, and the results were disastrous.

Eventually, Saul's heart was turned away from the Lord and the scriptures record that he had almost a beastly reaction to the prophetic anointing. (1 Samuel

Jonathan Ferguson

10:6-8; Samuel 13:10-14; Samuel 19:20-24). He also became abusive of his authority, which becomes typical of not only prophets, but also apostles alike who misappropriate the anointing on their lives. He no longer had authority over the devil in his own personal life and his public victories begin to pale in comparison to David's. Lastly, and most importantly, his expression of the prophetic was perverted, causing the people's perception of the prophetic to be distorted. In 1 Samuel 19:20-24, as the people observe Saul under the prophetic anointing, the thing they see the most is the nakedness of his flesh and they ask the question, "is Saul one of the prophets?"

  THERE ARE SOME QUESTIONS THAT NEED TO BE ANSWERED because there are many who have polluted and perverted the prophetic due to their flesh and their own personal sins. When people are hungry to see the move of God, they should not have to endure the nakedness of our flesh. The prophetic has gotten a bad name because it has been more about what we want rather than what God wants, but thank God that day is over. The prophetic is shifting. There will be many that rise who have a purity of prophetic flow and a fullness of prophetic expression in this coming shift, and you are reading this book in preparation for just that.

What is the Shift?

The reason I examined how Samuel anointed the first two kings of Israel is because I believe it is prophetically symbolic of how the kingdom and the prophetic work hand and hand. It all leads to this. I have found that people who truly understand the kingdom of God likewise understand the necessity for the institution of the prophet. Truth is, if we don't understand the kingdom, we will not understand the prophetic. And if we do not understand the prophetic, we will not understand the kingdom of God.

The two were being instituted in Israel through Samuel simultaneously for a reason, and its as we understand the kingdom that we will begin to understand the true order of the prophet. Many only understand the prophetic of what has been demonstrated in the church, which has even been limited in its true expression, yet God is shifting the prophetic in this season to return to its biblical roots and embrace its function in the kingdom more holistically. Over the last remaining chapters we will begin to investigate the true order of the prophet and begin to understand prophets from a kingdom perspective.

Chapter 7
The Prophet, World Systems, & Kingdom Dynamics

Chapter Objectives:
- Learn multiple dynamics of the Kingdom
- Understand the Kingdom mandate and the role of the prophet in executing it
- Understand world systems, various kingdoms of this world, and the mandate of the prophet to align them with the Kingdom of God
- Begin to understand the cultural impact of the prophet

Kingdom Dynamics:

The more we understand kingdom, the more we will understand order, authority, rank, protocol, and the supernatural power of God. They all are key in dealing with the prophetic. I want to take a brief moment to give you a basic overview.

Jonathan Ferguson

When kingdom comes, it enforces order and that's where we get into rank and protocol. Rank then comes to steward over the order in different measures. For example, apostles, prophets, teachers, evangelists, and pastors are the different measures of gifting and rankings that steward the order of the kingdom.

Next is where protocol and power come in to play. Protocol is rather how rank and order function together by making sure people don't cross boundaries, that they know their place, stay in it, and properly function in that place. Lastly, power without protocol doesn't last long, and it is self-destructive.

When we understand the previous truths, we will also understand that if the prophet is going to operate in the full measure of authority given to him in the kingdom, he must return to the original prophetic protocol. There is indeed a protocol pertaining to the measure of the kingdom that the prophet stewards. Protocol is the "how to," the "what to," or better put, the instruction manual.

Whenever the protocol is off, disorder will be the evidence. In other words, the proof that many who call themselves prophets are not legitimate is the confusion that is created as they operate in error. When we are not abiding by the "what to," "when to," or the "how to" of the prophetic, charismatic chaos is inevitable and many are confused in the process.

Prophets: 101

The problem is that many gravitate to the power of the prophetic while paying little attention to or having little knowledge concerning prophetic protocols. As we have previously understood, this is a violation of kingdom dynamics. In fact, it has been the very violation of certain protocols that have caused many to even reject the prophetic. However, the good news is that God is restoring order to the prophetic in this hour. He is raising up prophets that will steward the prophetic properly.

The Prophet and the Kingdom:

Now that we understand the prophet's responsibility to steward a measure of order in the kingdom, we should also begin to understand what it looks like to do so. This is important because when many think of a prophet they think "church" and not "kingdom." There are many who are called as prophets, but sadly their highest aspirations as prophets only consist of how much they preach in someone's pulpit. It's time we begin to understand the kingdom mandate of the prophet and just how much authority is extended to him so that he successfully stewards such an order. In order to do so, we must first understand the kingdom mandate.

The kingdom mandate is found in Revelations 11:15. It deals with the kingdoms of this world becoming the kingdoms of Christ. There are two key words in Revelations 11:15 that will help us better understand

Jonathan Ferguson

the nature of the kingdom in the text. The word "becoming" is the first key word in this text because it represents Jesus bringing the world back into divine alignment with heaven. The word "world" is another key word in Revelations 11:15.

The word "world" has great significance not only in Revelations 11:15, but throughout scripture that I believe many overlook. It's important we understand that the word "world" is translated from two different Greek words in scripture. One translation is from the Greek word "aeon," and it means culture. The second translation is from the Greek word "kosmos," and it means systems. If we are going to deal with kingdoms, we have to deal with culture, systems, various mountains of power, and various social stratas. We will explain this in more detail later in the remaining chapters, but there are some things we need to understand foundationally first.

The Foundation:

In Revelations 11:15, we should first notice that the word "kingdoms" is plural which means there are many kingdoms. Also, we should understand that there is a distinguishing between the many kingdoms and the kingdom of God. Let's briefly explain this truth. Buckle your seatbelts, please.

Matthew 6:10 talks about the kingdom of heaven, which of course is the highest and greatest kingdom.

In this text we are clearly instructed to pray that this kingdom comes in the earth. Within this kingdom there is an angelic kingdom. I don't want to go into detail about the angelic kingdom; however. I have a whole chapter written about the angelic kingdom and its structure in *Experiencing God in the Supernatural*.

Furthermore, Daniel 10:21 and Daniel 12:1 are proof that the angelic species is governed as a kingdom when it calls Michael, the archangel, a "prince." It's really simple—you don't need a prince if you don't have a king. And you don't need a king if you don't have a kingdom.

In addition to this, we can see the beginning of various kingdoms throughout all creation in the book of Genesis. In Genesis 1, we see how everything in the universe is created in order and in ranks. For example, Genesis 1:16 speaks of the greater lights and lesser light. And notice it says that one will rule the day and the other will rule the night, which is in fact the galactic kingdom. Even Genesis 1:21-25 speaks of animals according to their "kind," which is key because according to Revelations 1:5-7, whenever we are dealing with kindred and kinds we are dealing with kingdoms.

So far, we understand and have scripturally verified that there is an angelic kingdom, a galactic kingdom, and an animal kingdom. There are various kingdoms of this world (of men), and most important importantly, there is a kingdom of heaven. Now that

Jonathan Ferguson

this foundation is laid concerning understanding the reality of multiple kingdoms, I recommend the teachings of Dr. Cindy Trimm and Bishop Tudor Bismarck for further understanding and teaching of this subject. I only wanted to briefly lay a foundation so that I could bring you to the following point.

Among the kingdoms of men, there are multiple kingdoms of this world that operate in systems. These systems are the order of how the kingdom operates and functions. They are the institutions that shape our cultures and drive our progress as a civilization, which is where the prophetic becomes relevant because of the measure of order it stewards. The prophet affects every sphere of culture by aligning the kingdoms of this world with the Kingdom of heaven (Isaiah 3:2).

We will discuss some of these different spheres throughout the remainder of this book, yet I recommend the teachings of Lance Waulna concerning the "7 mountains" for a more exhaustive study on the subject. I will only deal with this subject enough for us to understand that there is a protocol to how the prophet is to function beyond the four walls of the church. Please be assured that although I am recommending other study material, I can guarantee you that you will have great understanding of these concepts by the time you complete this reading. Stay with me as I continue to lay a foundation that will be necessary to understand in order to grasp the key concepts throughout the remainder of this book.

Prophets: 101

Cultural Impact

Throughout the history of the prophets, God raised prophets up to impact the prominent spheres of culture of their day and time. For example, Daniel was a politician, while David impacted the music industry so strongly that it gave him access to the king's palace. In fact, many prophets were temple prophets who had their training as priests. This is significant because the temple for Israel's culture was not merely a religious culture, but it was connected heavily to the market and politics. It was a very public place. Temple prophets were very influential in the culture and/or had governmental positions and association.

The reason that it's important that prophets infiltrate cultures and systems is because prophets release the "next" moves of God. They have an anointing or are assigned to anoint individuals that will pioneer the forward progress of humanity in various social stratas and impact cultures. They have an anointing to not only see greatness in someone or something, but also to push into greatness or even impart it.

When the prophetic is in full expression, the church is not only relevant, but also ahead of its time. The prophetic causes innovation to come on people's lives. It anoints individuals to pioneer and trailblaze the cutting edge and the "never seen before." The order of the prophet that is being restored will so impact the culture that the church will once again become the leading influence in today's world and tomorrow's to come.

    Over the next chapter we are going to take time to more understand the world in which we live. We will understand where world systems and cultures have their origin in the plan of God. In doing so we will also understand the measure of authority that the prophet has both naturally and spiritually to bring reformation culturally, governmentally, nationally, and generationally.

Chapter 8
Culture and Prophetic Systems

Chapter Objectives:
- Understand the world we live in
- Discover the origin of world systems and various spheres of culture
- Learn what a prophetic system is, when it originated, and its three main historical pillars within Israel's culture
- Continue to understand the cultural impact of the prophet historically

If we are going to understand the impact the prophet has in a culture, we must better understand the world in which we live. As I aforementioned in the previous chapter, the word "world" is translated from the Greek words "kosmos" and "aeon", which are defined as culture and systems. Let's now take a deeper look at the word "kosmos", and in the final chapter, we will take a deeper look at the word "aeon." In doing so, we will better understand the world we live in and how the prophetic anointing impacts it.

Jonathan Ferguson

Kosmos is defined as systems or an ordered arrangement. In fact, the Greek word is not only defined as systems, but also one of the actual English equivalents of this word is "systems." For example, most nations have institutions of government, economics, education, etc. that are referred to as systems. These systems are key concerning the overall make-up of our world. They are an "ordered arrangement" of institutions that shape our societies and drive the progress of humanity.

The next thing we should know is that the root word of kosmos is komiz(d)o, which means "to provide for". This means that these systems not only make up our world, but are also designed "to provide for" the optimum earth experience. In fact, these systems are derived from key values of life that God instituted when He created Adam in the garden.

For example, we can see the origin of the family and social system when God said, "it is not good for man to be alone". In Genesis 2:11, even economics originated in the beginning at the Pison River, where there was gold. And the list goes on and on.

When God told us to be fruitful and multiply, He was letting us know that we would develop and advance. This is how these systems eventually came about. In other words, we can understand from the previous two examples that if money and family were not important to God, the social and economic systems would not exist.

These systems can also be referred to as social stratas, higher powers, institutions, pillars, and molders of culture. They are most frequently known as kingdoms and mountains. Some say that there are seven mountains; others say that there are ten kingdoms, while others say there are twelve. However, pinpointing the exact number and naming of the systems is not as important as is the ability to understand the concept.

The concept is that this is how our world functions. This is life as we know it and as God created it. God gave us life and placed us in a sphere where there was government, prosperity, family, recreation, education, and every other provision we needed in order to advance and have the optimum earth experience. As we understand this, we will understand the kingdoms of this world.

We should also understand that when we hear about seven mountains, twelve kingdoms, and other various terminologies, all of these variations are speaking of "the universe at large." It is a universe made up of the heavens and the earth, including various world systems and cultures. We should embrace the concept, understanding that this is how God created our world to function.

Jonathan Ferguson

The kingdoms of this world that Revelations 11:15 speak of are where world systems and their various spheres of culture fit into the universe at large. Although it is a very complex reality, I believe you are grasping the concept and will continue to as we progress. However, as we go deeper in our study, I want to remind and encourage you to research teaching on the seven mountains by Lance Walnau and teachings by Dr. Cindy Trimm and Bishop Tudor Bismarck on kingdoms.

Intro to Prophetic Systems:

The reason I laid a foundation in understanding world systems is so that we could understand the concept of prophetic systems. This is important because the historical account of Israel's culture has the prophet at the infrastructure. In other words, according to Isaiah 3:1-4, specifically vs. 2, the institution of the prophet did not just "impact systems," but it was a "system" in and of itself and had a key role in the development of Israel's various other key systems such as economics, government, etc. I call this a Prophetic System and I believe if we understand what this is, we can understand the historical cultural impact of the prophet.

There are some systems that originated in Eden as we have previously seen and there are others that originated after man's fallen state. We see this beginning with Cain and even tracing to Nimrod, who originated the Babylonian system. In fact, it was because

Prophets: 101

of the fall of man that some of these world systems became demonically inspired. It is also because of this that certain systems in certain nations are not as prominent as others. For example, the educational system in China is more prominent than the educational system of America.

With this in mind we should understand that the nation of Israel had a system in place that was not represented at any other nation. This is one reason why the exact numbering and terminologies of various systems, mountains, kingdoms, and spheres of culture are not as important as grasping the concept of how they function. This particular system that was scripturally represented in Israel that was not in any other nation is what I call the prophetic system. It is the system that was instituted by the prophet, at the infrastructure of Israel's culture, and was key to the success of every other part of Israel's society. Many have not heard of such a system, yet Isaiah 3:1-4 speaks of the validity of such a system.

In verse two of Isaiah 3, as the scriptures mention the leadership positions of various key spheres of culture, the prophet was one of them. This is how we know that in Israel, just as there were economic, educational, and governmental systems, there was also a prophetic system. I would like to take the remainder of this chapter to explain this prophetic system and how it functioned in Israel. In doing so, we will understand the order of the prophet in different eras. We will also understand the various leadership roles assigned to the office. Lastly, we will better understand the assignments of various historical prophets and what impact they had in the culture.

Prophetic Systems

The prophetic system began with a deliverer and a movement. When Moses was sent by God to bring Israel out of Egypt, it could be likened to a civil rights movement or political uprising with God backing it by signs and wonders following the message that Moses was given. This movement eventually transitioned and began to be governed by a judicial system, and later there was a transition into the Davidic Kingdom. From the time that God had first spoken to Abraham, and beyond the time that Moses led Israel out of Egypt, the prophetic was very key in the establishing of Israel's kingdom.

Judges 17:6 says something powerful about the times prior to the Kingdom of Israel being established. It speaks of how the people attempted to do as they pleased because there was no king yet in Israel. However, in those days, God raised up judges to govern Israel from among whom prophets would at times emerge. I believe that this era represents how the prophetic anointing even governed Israel until the days that Samuel established the Davidic kingdom.

Prophets: 101

The Davidic kingdom consisted of three pillars: king, priest, and prophet (1 Kings 1:32; 2 Samuel 24:11; 1 Chronicles 29:29). This infrastructure is historically the most prominent in Israel and if we understand this, we will understand prophetic systems. I believe the three pillars of King, Priest, and Prophet were key in establishing Israel as a "superpower" nation. Likewise, if America is going to continue to advance as a prosperous nation, it will need authentic prophetic voices.

The very essence of authentic prophetic anointing was continually demonstrated throughout Israel's culture through these three pillars of Israel's society with no other agenda but to bring alignment with heaven. The prophetic system within these three pillars of Israel shows us how the prophet's role would adjust to accommodate the social system he was called to impact. There was no part of Israel's livelihood that the prophetic did not impact or influence. We will understand this as we examine the prophetic within each pillar of the Davidic kingdom, which are as follows: Priest, Prophet, and King.

1st Pillar: The Priest

It is no surprise how at times God would raise up priests as prophets, as we understand how the Levitical priesthood began with a prophet by the name of Aaron. In fact, often times the priesthood would be the training grounds for the budding prophet. Samuel is a great example of such and also an example of how at times

Jonathan Ferguson

God would bring correction to the Priesthood through the prophet as seen in the life of Ezekiel as well. The key in understanding the significance of how the priesthood and prophetic are intertwined is in understanding that the temple had a very influential presence in the culture of the Jews.

    I reiterate, the Temple was not revered as merely a religious institution or symbol, but it was connected heavily to the market and politics. It was a very public place and completely different than how the religious system operates today. Temple prophets were very influential in the culture and often times had key governmental association. In fact, at one point in history, a king was not even legitimate if had not been anointed by the priest, which leads to next pillar of this Davidic kingdom.

2nd Pillar: The King

    We must remember that a king would not exist in Israel if it were not for the prophet Samuel. It is more historically significant than many credit that the prophet Samuel anointed the first two kings. It is likewise no coincidence that prophets would often be hired as the king's seer, which was the king's number one advisor as we have also previously discussed. If you have not read chapters three and four, I encourage you to go back and read. The offices of priest, prophet, and king were so intertwined that David is remembered as one who occupied all three. He is often remembered as prophet, priest, and king; after all, this system is patterned after his rule and reign in the kingdom.

3rd Pillar: The Prophet

The origin of how the prophetic school was established has given us great insight into how important prophetic expression was to Israel's culture. We should further understand from this reality that prophets were rarely seen in the public's eye as "solo acts." Prophets would often associate and partner with a company of prophets among a school of the prophets. Senior prophets among this school were responsible for training successive prophets who would eventually have a similar influence in ultimately shaping the culture of the nation around kingdom moral and principles.

Even Elijah, although he suddenly shows up in the scriptures without any reference to his lineage, was not superior to this order of the prophet. The scriptures indicate of Elijah and how he later functioned as the one who was appointed over the company of prophets that Samuel had once established. Every prominent prophet was recognized by some type of authority, which is why an authentic calling as an apostle or prophet does not exempt one from submission. In fact, it rather puts more emphasis on the need for accountability.

The prophetic was highly recognized, respected and credentialed. This is one of the reasons that I

Jonathan Ferguson

believe Jesus mentioned receiving a prophet in the name of a prophet. In other words, the prophetic was so highly respected that even if a certain prophet was not highly exposed in the public's eye, the prophet was still to be received as long as they had the endorsement of another more recognized prophet. Even if the prophet was yet to be well known or influential, it was very disrespectful to neglect the prophet because of how necessary he is and was to the prosperity of a people.

Conclusion

I believe the Davidic kingdom represents a prophetic system because of how the prophets of old either had key and influential leadership roles, or they had some type of history within the previous three pillars. However, the prophets were yet often misunderstood. In fact, the very ones that actually somewhat understood the prophets were the ones that resisted them the most. Jesus Himself spoke of how the prophets were beaten, slandered, and assassinated by the unrighteous and the rebellious. I believe this is because although the prophets played a key role in the origin of the nation of Israel, they were never called to fit into the system.

Prophets have always been called by God to infiltrate world systems in order to make sure that they remain in alignment with heaven. God in His understanding knew that if He allowed the prophet to become too comfortable in the system, they would never "buck the system" when it was necessary for them to do so. In the next chapter I will explain what I mean by "bucking the system" and how this both creates and maintains Kingdom culture.

Chapter 9
Shifting Power Systems

Chapter Objectives:
- Understand what a power shifts are and how prophets initiate them
- Understand the importance of the supernatural in the ministry of the prophet
- Understand how God causes governmental authorities to submit to the counsel of the prophets when major shifts need to take place
- Begin to understand how prophets deal with demonic principalities and powers and how prophets must follow up afterward in order to maintain victory

We have learned according to the book of Revelations that the Kingdoms of this world are becoming the kingdoms of our God and Christ. This means that the world we live in is being brought back into alignment with the kingdom of heaven. This also means that the ministry of the prophet has an ability to affect every sphere of culture by the measure of order it is called to steward in the kingdom.

Jonathan Ferguson

It means that as prophets govern and bring order, they cause divine alignment. They monitor what's taking place in the earth to make sure that it reflects what heaven intends and mandates for it. Let's take the time to see exactly what that looks like in order to continue understanding the impact the prophetic has on the culture.

Bucking the Systems

One of the primary ways that prophets bring divine alignment is by infiltrating world powers and bucking their systems. Let me explain. "Bucking" is a word used to describe a resistance or opposition. It also means "to find a way" or "proceed against." When the church seems to lose it's relevance and significance in a culture, we should always be aware that God is yet looking for ways to show Himself strong.

When prophets discern that systems are being demonically driven, they do two things to alter them. First, they buck systems to intercept demonic agendas, ultimately causing major powers to shift. Next, they raise up new leadership who engage the world in order to raise the standard of righteousness and create kingdom culture.

In other words, the people must be called back to righteousness and new leaders must emerge. In the next chapter, we will explain the concept of raising new leadership in more detail. But first let's take the time to examine the process by which prophets cause major powers to shift.

The importance of Signs and Wonders

In order to buck power systems and bring divine alignment, prophets rely heavily on the ministry of signs and wonders. To understand this, we must first understand what I mean by power systems. Romans 13:1 mentions "higher powers" to describe ruling governmental and social powers.

The ruling governments were also referenced in the text as the "powers that be." In fact, Romans 13:1 is speaking of the same concept that we have previously expounded on pertaining to world systems, institutions, social stratus, mountains, and more. In addition to the previous, I would also like to refer to this reality as power systems, world powers, major powers, or major power systems in reference to the authorities that govern culture.

One reason that the ministry of signs and wonders so impacts culture is because of the attention it draws. Scriptures speak a lot about how multitudes would travel on foot from city to city just to see Jesus, hear the Word, and see the miracles (Luke 5:15; Luke 6:17). Scriptures also speak of how His fame spread and how individuals of great authority and influence would seek Him out (Luke 5:17).

Jonathan Ferguson

Signs and wonders have always proven to have a strong influence on the majority because of how people will never get enough of seeing others healed, delivered, and raised from the dead. It will always leave individuals in awe and will never lose its significance. In fact, it was the miraculous that validated Jesus as a prophet in the eyes of the Jews, because of how they were accustomed to the prophets of old demonstrating the supernatural power of God.

Signs and wonders have always been a very intricate part of prophetic ministry. It was through the ministry of the prophet that the dead were raised, the sick were healed, and even wars were won. Weather patterns were adjusted, the laws of physics were broken, and even time itself was altered. When things like this take place, people begin to realize that there is a power above the "powers that be" (Romans 13:1).

However, there is yet more understanding concerning the ministry of signs and wonders needed in order for us to have more clarity concerning the ministry of the prophet. In addition to the miraculous being made evident to bless an individual's personal life, the ministry of signs and wonders can facilitate the judgments of God and also bend the laws of nature.

Prophets yield great power in the previous two areas causing a chain reaction of events that can alter various national institutions and power systems. It is as we understand this that we better understand the prophet's cultural influence. Let's look at the reality of how prophets initiate the judgments of God and bend laws of nature and somewhat examine each factor.

The Judgments of God:

Many confuse the wrath of God and the judgment of God. The wrath of God is His anger or punishment, yet the judgments of God are his assessments and evaluations. When God judges a thing, He weighs it and if it is off balance, there are actions that can be taken to restore the balance. He does this because the scripture says that a false balance is an abomination.

In most cases the actions that God takes in a judgment are aimed at one of the following two primary targets. One, according to John 12:30-31 and John 16:9, 11, judgment can be targeted in ways to disarm and overthrow demonic principalities and powers (Luke 10:17; Ephesians 2:1-6). Secondly, judgment can be targeted through temporary hardships in ways that position us in a place where our assessment of life and our worldviews are brought back into agreement with heaven's agenda.

If there is a case in which both demonic powers and the people of the land are equally involved in transgressing the land, God has a remedy. He will allow those of us who rely upon this world's systems to be faced with issues that only He can answer. As a result we are placed in positions in which we are open to heed the counsel of God through His prophets. When this takes place, it is usually not a punishment, but rather a repositioning strategy and tactic.

When a people come into agreement with an evil spirit that wants to govern a nation or generation, God simply lifts His hand so that the people begin to see that their conditions are not so favorable after all without Him (2 Chronicles 7:14). Prophets are then able to step in and offer counsel either regarding repentance or forward advancement. The story of Joseph's counsel to Pharaoh, and Daniel's counsel to the Babylonian and Persian kings are great examples of this truth.

However, if the judgments of God are not heeded, they can in fact become the wrath of God. It was the judgments of God that released Peter out of King Herod's prison. However, it was the wrath of God that sent the angel to slay Herod after he resisted the judgments of God and did not give God His glory (Acts 12).

It was the judgment of God that sentenced Nebuchadnezzar to seven years of insanity. However, the son of Nebuchadnezzar did not repent after the judgment of his father. Therefore, it was the wrath of God through the writing on the wall that revealed how the son of Nebuchadnezzar would be given over to destruction by the hands of the Medes and the Persians (Daniel 4:24-37; Daniel 5:5-31).

Prophets: 101

You should notice though previous examples that the judgments of God are not always disciplinary and the wrath of God is not always necessary. Furthermore, prophets do not command the judgments of God, but they instead facilitate them. Their presence brings the balance that it necessary; however, they are on the contrary required to express the heart of God towards people in mercy and compassion, less the judgments of God be upon them.

Bending Laws and Elements of Nature:

Just as Jesus walked on water, walked through walls, and transported Himself instantly to different locations, prophets have always had an incredible way of bending the laws of physics and nature (Matthew 14:25; John 20:26). For example, when Joshua spoke the sun, time stood still (Joshua 10:12-14). When Isaiah prophesied, time went backwards (Isaiah 38:5-8).

Elijah at multiple times called fire out of heaven (1 Kings 18:36-38; 2 Kings 1:10-14). In fact, both Elijah and Samuel even controlled weather patterns (1 Samuel 12:16-18; 1 Kings 17:1; 1 Kings 18:41-46). Moses parted waters, while Elisha halted food poison epidemics (2 Kings 4:40-44).

As prophets of old demonstrated the supernatural, they were not mere novice shows of power, but carried the potential to and at times did in fact dramatically alter the state of world systems. We only understand how this is possible as we remember our study on the root word for the Greek word kosmos (world systems). The root is word komidzo, which means "provision."

This means that every world system has a provision, whether it is a natural resource that is allocated to it or a key moral value that governs its social quality. These provisions were embedded into creation itself and necessary to the basic functioning and advancing of various world systems. For example, without knowledge there can be no educational system.

Without family and relationships, there would be no social system. Without the commandment, there would be no governmental system. And without commodity resources and land produce, there would be no economic system.

Understanding the story of Elijah and how he stopped the rain is a great illustration that will help us understand the previous truths (1 Kings 17:1). When Elijah commanded that it not rain for the space of three years, it had tremendous effect on the land's ability to harvest, which subsequently caused a famine. The rain was connected to the land, the land was connected to the harvest, and the harvest was connected to the economy. Elijah literally shifted the economic systems of every nation and the economic status of everyone living during that era by bending the laws of nature.

Prophets: 101

Power Shifts:

Prophets exercise authority over world systems and major ruling powers of men by a mixture of their nabi, shamar, nataph functions that we covered in chapter three. Therein, we learned that prophets are climate changers. They create and govern atmospheres as they spiritually police environments and territories.

As gatekeepers, they determine what's coming in and what's going out. Furthermore, by the Issachar anointing they know what should be done and strategically when to do it. Thereby, they are equipped to ensure forward progress of a nation or people.

It would be novice of us to think that all of this power is packed into an individual for no other purpose but to give random prophetic words. Likewise, it is almost impossible to understand the things we have come to learn so far throughout this book and not take on more of a kingdom of God type of worldview in light of the prophetic. The prophet's mantle is no doubted uniquely wired for the purposes of shifting major world-power systems that align themselves with demonic entities. Prophets shift ruling powers ultimately causing them to accommodate the plans of God in the earth.

Prophets do not bow to the demonic powers of the air that Ephesians 2:2 speak of. In fact, although we are to obey the governmental "powers that be", prophets have been given authority by God to confront them if they compromise the truths of God's word. When prophets speak into atmospheres and speak to people of authority, major powers begin to shift. The governing bodies of even the universe are altered. Prophets are like spiritual governors and mayors who govern and function in ways where they do not obey the system but the system obeys them. This is what I mean by " bucking the system".

The prophets were the first to buck the system. They did not only create a kingdom culture at the infrastructure of Israel's existence, but they have also been empowered by God to maintain and expand that culture in the earth. Prophets have it in them to instinctively be at odds with anything that threatens the laws, morality, principles, and ethics of the Kingdom of God. When there is a demonic influence within a political or social party, prophets are empowered to challenge them.

Prophets do not submit to any form of government, social trend, or system that is opposed to the Kingdom of God. As ambassadors of Christ, their job is to acclimate the territory that they are assigned to with the Kingdom culture of heaven. Therefore, the laws that govern the ministry of the prophet are superior to even the laws of physics, affording them the ability to challenge major world powers that attempt to defy the will of God in the earth. When prophets speak, what they say comes to pass. When they move, the entire universe adjusts to accommodate their existence.

Conclusion

By now you should have an incredible sense of the kingdom dynamics that will help you view the prophetic from a completely different perspective. Everything you have read in the first five chapters has a completely new relevance. And over the next chapter, we will continue this thought and examine how prophets intercept demonic agendas as major powers are adjusted. We will also examine why it is necessary that new leadership begin to emerge once a movement of that magnitude takes place. Once you finish the next chapter, which is the final chapter, you will have reached the point of no return. In fact, you have already reached that point and now there is no turning back. You will never view the prophetic in the way that you previously have.

Chapter 10
Emerging Leaders

Chapter Objectives:
- Understand the importance of next generation leaders emerging after cultures are altered prophetically
- Cross-reference the current prophetic movement with the confrontation of Elijah against Ahab and Jezebel
- Understand the stages and dangers of moral decline
- Understand Jezebel's lineage, the origin of the Babylonian system, how world systems began to be demonically influenced, and how it all parallels to our current culture
- Understand how the spiritual climate in the eras of Elijah, Noah, and Daniel parallel
- Understand generational breakthroughs and how prophets conquer demonic principalities and powers
- Understand changing times and how all believers play a part in prophetically reforming cultures

Jonathan Ferguson

Intro

Since you have made it this far, I will let you in on a little secret. I'm sure that you have noticed that not everything I mention from the Bible has the scriptural reference included. Your homework is to go research the scriptural references that were not included. After all, this book is called *Prophets 101*. I once heard it said that it is almost impossible to teach transformation revelation to individuals who do not read their Bibles. There is not much mentioned in this book at all that does not reference a biblical story or scriptural truth. The biblical confirmation will only enhance the significance of your studies as you also discover that you will only be as prophetically comprehensive as you are biblically literate. Now let's continue our final chapter studies.

We ended the previous chapter dealing with how prophets are equipped to shift major power systems. We also learned reasons why after prophets shift major power systems, they must next raise up the next generation of leaders who engage the culture. When I began to understand this revelation, I better understood Elijah's conflict with Jezebel. We are going to look at this story as we conclude this book, and I believe there is going to be yet another paradigm shift concerning the prophetic as a result. We are going to raise the standard concerning what authentic prophetic expression is, and we are going to raise up a generation of prophetic people who create contagious kingdom culture.

Dealing with Jezebels

In the process of establishing a kingdom culture, a prophet will find that he will always confront a Jezebel. It is important to thoroughly understand this conflict because of the less obvious realities of her work against the kingdom of God. The obvious that is understood of Jezebel is that she was a witch. The less obvious is how her witchcraft was aimed at controlling government and controlling prophetic expression.

Whenever there is not an authentic expression of the prophetic, it is evident that Jezebel is in operation, which is one reason why Elijah historically came on the scene out of nowhere. The scriptures do not speak about his lineage or where he was born, and he didn't have any association with the current prophetic movements or prophets in the land.

Elijah comes to set things straight and restore order to the prophetic movement. And he is successful in that he is later seen appointed over the school of the prophets that Samuel had instituted. As a result, Elijah becomes the new standard of prophetic expression, which is one reason I believe the scriptures speak concerning the spirit of Elijah. I want to warn you that you will need to buckle your seatbelt as this truth unfolds layer by layer.

Jonathan Ferguson

Where Elijah Went Wrong and How He Corrected It

When Elijah goes into a depression after Jezebel threatens him, God says to him that there is a prophetic remnant of seven thousand. I believe that this remnant had to do with the sons of the prophets who were apart of the school and company that Samuel had instituted. God was reminding Elijah of where true prophetic expression in its fullness had begun with Samuel establishing a school prior to the prophetic eventually branching off into the government (seers). Even though the prophetic had gradually formed political ties that eventually led to perversion, there was still yet a remnant of prophetic voices among the school of the prophets.

I had always wondered why after Elijah had called fire down out of heaven, Jezebel was still a threat to him. The Lord showed me that after Elijah dried up the economy by stopping the rain, and shook the religious institutions after calling down fire, there was still a need to infiltrate the government and purify the prophetic that was represented in the government. If Elijah was going to successfully deal with Jezebel, he was going to also deal with the source of her power, which was Ahab's governmental position.

Just as in the days of Elijah, there is now a need for authentic prophetic voices and expression because although our ministries are successful, our cities and our governments are not being changed. This is evidence that there is still demonic activity in high places that needs to be dealt with and thanks to God that can be overcome. There is a prophetic movement emerging that will overthrow demonic powers in high places.

Dealing with Jezebels and Ahabs

More so than witchcraft, Jezebel also represented demonic activity in high and influential places. Today there are occults that partner with governments, witches that infiltrate churches, and all kinds of evils that keep our cities and nations in bondage. However, everyone has seemed to focus on Jezebel, yet ignoring the fact that there can be no Jezebel without an Ahab.

It is Ahab that represents weak and compromising leaders and leadership. Many leaders even in the church sell their souls for fame and fortunes given by demonic assistance. The only way to effectively rid of this is to raise up the next generation of leadership.

This is the revelation that Elijah was given in the cave. Not only did Elijah connect to the company of prophets that Samuel instituted, but he also was given an assignment to anoint three key future leaders after his cave experience. Elijah was discouraged because He didn't understand how Jezebel was still coming against him after all the miracles.

Jonathan Ferguson

He had yet to understand that after the kingdom comes and impacts cultures and nations with the miracles and preaching of the gospel, there is a need to engage the culture. This is one reason Jesus told the Apostles to make sure they occupy and do business until He returns. It is after major powers and demonic authorities are dislodged that the church must occupy those positions of influence ensuring that lawlessness does not return.

Miracles in a Backslidden Culture

In the previous chapter, we learned that miracles are usually involved in the first stages of infiltrating power systems that are demonically controlled because of the kingdom impact they have. However, after the initial impact, new leadership must be raised up to engage the culture. Our present problem is that we attempt to engage culture without the miracles first and it just doesn't work.

I encourage every reader to read a teaching on "the finger of God" in chapter four *of Experiencing God in the Supernatural* in order to better understand this truth. If we are going to properly and effectively engage culture, we must first acknowledge that the power of God is still relevant today. However, if there is no follow up after the miraculous power of God impacts a people, we can end up losing the ground we have gained.

Matthew 12:43-45 says that when a spirit goes out, it comes back with seven more worse if there is no follow up. The revelation is that when Jesus made this statement it was not in context of an individual's deliverance, but in context of a rebuke that was in reference to an entire generation that refused to believe in the signs that were demonstrated through Him (Matthew 12:22-45). Notice that in Matthew 12:22-45 Jesus rebukes the Pharisees for seeking a sign, yet in John 10:37-38, He tells his followers not to believe Him unless He shows a sign.

The two are not contradictory. The individuals in John 10 were not rejecting the power of God and they were believing on Jesus. However, the individuals in Matthew 12 wanted Jesus to prove himself to them while ignoring the signs that He had already demonstrated. Therefore, in Matthew 12:43-45, Jesus warns them concerning the result that their rebellion would have on their generation.

It is also interesting that the rebuke of Matthew 12:22-45 carried a similar tone of the rebuke that Jesus gave to cities that did not repent after they had seen the miracles (Luke 10:8-16). Jesus was warning that when a generation sees His power and there is no proper response or follow up, the state of the people actually becomes worse. The city of Samaria is a great example of this truth.

Jonathan Ferguson

In John 4 it was in Samaria that the "woman at the well" brought the whole city out to meet Jesus, yet not even a whole generation later in Acts 8, the same city is under the power of sorcery. I believe this is why when Philip went to Samaria and the whole city was impacted again, he was prompted by God to implement a follow up plan. Philip called for Peter to join him in Samaria, and as a result the people were filled with the Spirit and discipled so that they would be less likely to backslide the second time around. The wisdom is that once a nation or generation is impacted by the power of God, proper leadership must be set in place in order to progress the culture forward or it will automatically go backward again.

More on Elijah and Jezebel

Now going back to the story of Elijah, we should better understand what was taking place in his conflict with Jezebel. The reason that Jezebel was yet to be defeated is because Elijah had only begun the process of infiltration through demonstrating God's power in the economic and religious systems. God wanted him to next begin to release the prophetic anointing in the lives of individuals who would assume leadership positions and further engage the culture.

This is not something to be taken lightly. If we are going to engage culture, we have to be strategic and there are some key things we should understand. For one, we should know that a culture is only as strong as its morality, which majority of the time is shaped by what is seen and heard. This is why mass communications are key in shaping a culture. In particular, media is effective because it reinforces what you see and hear at the same time.

However, before there was media, the only way the prophet could have cultural impact was through the visibility and constant exposure of prophetic expression. This is one reason why Jezebel wanted to pervert the prophetic. She knew if she could hinder authentic prophetic expression, she could cause a moral breakdown and cause the culture to be demonically influenced. I believe this is perfect place to dive into some research concerning Jezebel's lineage so that we can better understand what demonic forces Elijah was facing in that particular culture. In doing so, we will better understand some of the demonic plots that are being set us against our present culture and how to deal with them prophetically.

Jezebel's Lineage & Moral Decline

One of the last signs of moral breakdown prior to judgment is the continual increase in sexual perversions, according to Genesis 18 and19 and Romans 1 and 2. In fact, this is another thing that Jezebel was known for: fornication (Revelations 2:20). What many do not understand is that Jezebel is from the lineage of Nimrod who is believed historically to have originated

Jonathan Ferguson

idol worship and also known scripturally to have orchestrated the beginning of the Babylonian system.

Nimrod is known as the man who attempted to revive an evil that spawned in the days of Noah prior to the flood. The history of the previous facts are significant in that in Noah's day, fallen angels began to breed with men, and in Nimrod's day it is believed that men had begun to worship them. Nimrod could very well be the origin of what we understand concerning Greek mythology (Acts 27:27-34; Acts 19:34-38).

One of the primary false gods that Nimrod and the people of Babylon historically worshiped was a god that was fashioned after a fish. The type of fish in particular that the idolatry was fashioned after would mate with male and female fish, which of course represents same sex relations. This false god is also believed to have eventually become known as the idol Dagon that the Philistines worshipped. In fact, the demonic activity of the Philistines, Nimrod, and Sodom is all directly intertwined with people who lived during the days of Noah and during the days of Elijah.

Furthermore, it is very interesting the scriptures often mention the sexual immorality of Sodom in context of fallen angels and their activity during the days of Noah (Genesis 6:1-4; Jude 6-7; 2 Peter 2:4-9). In doing so, the scriptures prophetically track the timeline of demonic activity throughout multiple eras. The fact is that the activities of Nimrod, his seed Jezebel,

Prophets: 101

the Philistines, and Sodom all represent the existence of long-standing demonic principalities and powers that prophets are called to confront. We will explain these parallels more shortly, but first let's understand that when these types of demonic powers are in operation, it reflects in the quality of the culture. There is a pattern in this that includes the same sex agenda, the breakdown of the family, and the influence of demonic authorities within the culture.

In particular, when a culture begins to promote the same sex agenda, it is a sign that the particular culture is at the last stages of moral decay. It's also important to understand that this activity is ultimately an attack on the family structure, which is both the foundation of social stability and one of the last lines of defense in a moral collapse. Once there is a moral collapse, world systems become almost completely demonically driven. Furthermore, when a system is demonically driven, the culture begins to accommodate the personality of evil spirits instead of hosting the presence of God.

It is important to understand the previous information serves as a foundation in realizing the ramifications of the prophetic conflict with Jezebel that we are examining. As we continue to reference the opposition of Jezebel towards Elijah, we will realize the relevance it has pertaining to the current prophetic movement that is emerging in the earth. Truth is, God wants habitation in cities and regions, and that requires authentic apostolic and prophetic expression according to Ephesians 2:20-22, which is exactly what Jezebel wanted to do away with as we have previously learned.

However, when prophets enter a city or nation, they deal with the demonic authorities that want to control the systems of this world. As I have aforementioned, prophets deal with the powers of the air, and they shift those powers in the heavens. Sophisticated demons that operate behind politics are exposed. Demonic strongholds are taken and plundered so that spiritual climates can be adjusted. It is as the prophets of God return to this mandate that the kingdom of God will once again invade regions and nations. We will expound on this more in a moment, but first let's further examine the prophetic parallels of Noah's day, Sodom, Jezebel, and more.

Prophetic Parallels

Jesus said that it would be in the end times as it was in the days of Noah. We often fail to realize key truths concerning that statement because we fail to realize how it was in the days of Noah. The scriptures say that the imaginations of men's hearts were continually evil (Genesis 6:5). In order to understand what this means, we have to look at what Jesus teaches concerning what an evil heart looks like in Matthews 15:19. When we do so, we discover a staggering truth. The interesting fact is that Matthew 15:19 doubles in how much it references sexual immorality to an evil heart in comparison to every other vice mentioned.

This is important because many have come to compromise in their thoughts concerning sexual immorality. Often we fail to realize that the activity of such is in reality the indicator of more strategic workings of the demonic world behind the scenes. Sexual perversion is a key sign that demons are attempting to dominate high and influential places.

In fact, almost always, when idolatry is mentioned in scripture, it is linked with sexual immorality. This is very significant in that idolatry represents more than the worship of false gods. It actually also scripturally represents the worship of demons or fallen angels (1 Corinthians 10:14-23). It was in fact the worship of fallen heavenly entities, which takes us back to the days of Noah.

The days of Noah represent a significant moral decline in history that would repeat itself. It represents an origin of an evil that continues to propagate its agenda throughout successive generations. Let's not forget what the scriptures indicate how during the days of Noah that fallen angels began to have sexual intercourse with men, which created a hybrid species (Genesis 6:1-4; Jude 6-7; 2 Peter 2:4-9).

Scriptures say that because of this there were men of renown and giants in those times and in the times afterward, which is where the Philistines originated. It is no coincidence that these giants known as Philistines worshiped a god similar to the one that it is believed that Nimrod began to worship as I mentioned earlier. Are you following the parallels? If you are not, go back and read the last couple of pages again. If you are following the parallels—good. Now let's go deeper.

Jezebel, Nimrod, & the Babylonian System

It is believed that when these fallen angels rebelled and slept with men in an attempt to block the bloodline (seed/DNA) of Christ, that they taught men a couple of things. It is believed that idol worship was taught along with sexual perversions and advanced technologies. If this is accurate, it explains how God himself said that Nimrod was going to be able to build a tower that reached the heavens (Genesis 11).

After all, it would require very advanced technology considering the fact that we are still now thousands of years later trying to figure out better ways to explore Mars alone. Men to this day are still trusting in science and technology to find an alternative means to eternal life. This is one of the things that the tower that Nimrod was leading in constructing represented. Now don't get me wrong, science and technology are great as long as they are not used in attempts to be substitutions for God.

Prophets: 101

The scriptures say that God called the place where they were building the tower "babel," which means confusion. Babel became the foundation of what we call the Babylonian system. This explains why in the book of Deuteronomy, when God warns Israel of homosexuality, He tells them that it is "confusion."

In other words, God was teaching them that this type of sexually confused activity originated in the Babylonian system. God is pointing back to the place where fallen angels first slept with men and created giants. This also explains why when angels were sent to rescue Lot and his family out of Sodom, the men of Sodom wanted to sleep with the angels. I wonder if Noah would have been able to explain to Lot where the men of Sodom got this bright idea? I think you get the point now.

When Jesus talked about the days of Noah in the last days, we should more so understand by now of everything that is included. I reiterate that Jesus is in actuality partly referencing demonic forces that have been working over time through the ages in attempts to restore the satanic regime that began in the days of Noah and attempted to resurface in the days of Nimrod, from which the lineage of Jezebel began. This is why in different eras, various factors of this dark plot are evident.

The only difference in Elijah's conflict with Jezebel is how this evil personified as a woman much like how

Jonathan Ferguson

Isaiah 47:1-5 speaks of Babylon and the lady of the kingdom. This is also very similar to how Paul was in conflict with the goddess of Diana. In fact, Acts 19:34-37 says that the people worshiped both the goddess Diana and the image that was believed to have fallen from Jupiter. Hold up. Wait. Pause.

Are you serious, from Jupiter? You mean to tell me that alien myths are old news and centered around this prophetic conflict with Jezebel also? With all of the previous facts in mind, it shouldn't be a surprise why there is rapid advancement of technology, growing suspicion of aliens, growing support of same sex agenda, rising interest in occult and Greek mythology, and the demoralizing of the church. It is time for the prophets to rise and restore balance, bring correction, and raise the standard of holiness in our current cultures.

Emerging Prophetic Leaders in a Babylonian System

The good news is that God is raising up some powerful prophetic leaders in these last days. In fact, there are two things that we know for sure that are relevant to this teaching that are going to take place in the end times. One, we know that there is going to be a worldwide prophetic movement (Acts 2:17). Secondly, we know that this Babylonian system that Jezebel actually represented is going to fall.

Prophets: 101

We can rejoice in this fact because it is a sure thing. In the meantime, I believe God wants to show us how everything we have learned about how the prophetic mantle works to establish a Kingdom of God culture that defies demonic systems. We will do so as we conclude this chapter, and lastly, you will be inspired to find your place in this prophetic movement that is raising the standard of what prophetic ministry is all about.

In addition to Elijah, Noah, and Isaiah, Daniel is a great example of how to be in this Babylonian system and yet create a kingdom culture. All throughout the book of Daniel, he is infiltrating systems and bringing the kingdom of God in. He was constantly dealing with the demonic activity that was operating behind the scenes as his prayers conquered principalities and powers.

Likewise, prophets are called to dismantle demonic authorities. We have to be willing to speak with the enemy at the gate and know that the gates of hell will not prevail against us. This is one reason why prophets are called to confront sin.

Prophets understand the door that sin opens to the demonic, and as gate keepers, we are called to guard those entryways. Many may have cringed as I previously wrote about sexually immoralities, but you have to understand that I was writing as a gatekeeper and not a critical or judgmental person. Emerging leaders are not afraid to confront sin and deal with demonic authorities. It is as they step out in both love and boldness to do so that generations to come are preserved.

Generational Breakthroughs

Even in the life of Daniel, after the system was successfully infiltrated, there was a need for new leaders to emerge and engage culture. The famous account of Daniel's breakthrough over the prince of Persia is a great illustration of this truth. In one of Daniel's greatest victories, the angel came and told him that although the demonic prince of Persia was defeated, he was yet returning to war against the demonic prince of Greece.

Many miss an awesome revelation of what the angel was saying to Daniel. Let me show you. It was after Daniel had gotten the breakthrough over Persia that the angel then went back into the realm of the spirit and waged war for the future victory of God's people. The angel of the Lord was literally giving Daniel insight into the times to come and letting him know that he was giving him victory over "the demon of his future."

In order to better understand the significance, we must know that Greece was yet to be a super power at the time that Daniel had received the revelation of the prince of Greece. More specifically, Greece was the actual governmental super power prior to the Roman government that was set up during the days of Jesus. This is such an awesome revelation because of the fact that there were so many generations in between Daniel's present victory and the future victory that the angel was going back into the realm of the spirit to retrieve. In other words, Daniel was so powerful in the spirit that generations after him, leading all the way up to the birth of Jesus, benefited from his victory.

The revelation of the prince of Persia and the prince of Greece is that after there is breakthrough, there should be generational progress. For this reason, prophets are pioneers. They also anoint individuals that will pioneer the forward progress of humanity in various social stratas as culture evolves. Prophets can see the potential for greatness, promote one into greatness, or even impart the greatness depending on what's most necessary according to the changing times.

Aeons: Changing Times

We have previously understood how the word "Aeon" is one of the Greek words for the word "world." We have learned that Aeon deals with culture, yet we should further understand that it deals with time. Therefore, when dealing with culture we are dealing with seasons or time periods in which culture has to change.

Jonathan Ferguson

In other words, there are times that God orders, regardless of who is influencing the culture, that an element of change comes into fruition. If we do not prophetically discern these times, we allow the enemy to keep shaping the culture as it changes. However, if we as God's people will get in the midst of these ordained moments, prophetically we can get ahead of the time and begin to declare and establish how things are going to change and begin to see a new order emerging.

Whenever the times begin to change, God begins to give individuals ideas, goals, dreams, new anointing, and new vision. The key is in understanding that whenever God gives an individual vision, prophetic strategy is required in order to move forward in it. I believe there is a group of people who understand the times we live in and will prophetically seize the moment. These are they that God will use to raise the standard concerning what the prophetic represents in our culture. And there are others also who—through the prophetic anointing—will be empowered and positioned to redefine the culture itself.

I believe this is the hour that prophets are being strategically positioned by God to ensure that the enemy does not continue to dominate the culture and that all believers alike will discover their role in shaping tomorrow's world. And most importantly, I believe you have a part to play in this. You are not called to the sidelines in this movement. You are an emerging leader and you are called to raise the standard. You're anointed to "take it up a notch," and you are going to the next dimension in the prophetic.

What is in Your House?

There is always more to learn concerning the prophetic, but my assignment with this book was to introduce to you a concept that leads up to this point. There is so much more that has been covered and more that can be covered, but I would like to conclude with the famous question of Elisha to the widow woman: "what is in your house?" This is the question that activated and stirred up the prophetic potential inside of her. Whether you are called to be a prophet or not, God is placing a demand on the gifting inside of you because He wants to raise up a kingdom culture in this hour.

The prophetic is powerful not only in everything we've learned so far, but also partly because of how its revelation knowledge has the capacity to cause an individual to advance both spiritually and naturally. It is not something that is only activated at times when we feel most spiritual, but rather God's way of allowing us to access divine wisdom for every aspect of our lives. And this is something in which everyone can participate. If there is any anointing that should make the supernatural most practical and relevant in our lives, it is the prophetic. Therefore, it's time we start utilizing that prophetic anointing not only in the church, but also in the world around us.

Jonathan Ferguson

For example, I believe Steve Jobs' innovative success in the creation of the Apple company was prophetic in nature and could have been claimed by a believer. In reality, it doesn't matter how creative an individual is—it takes a prophetic anointing to make the "next" relevant and merge it with the "now." Just think what would happen when we, operating under the prophetic anointing, begin registering new businesses or maybe even teaching in universities.

What could happen if believers began to have more influence in how movies were directed and produced, or began to be the ones writing the scripts? I believe a prophetic people are about to rise up among athletes, sports commentators, news anchors, producers, CEOs, and bankers. We are about to rise among governors, kings, investigative reporters, research analysts, business consultants, comedians, bestselling authors, music artists and more.

I am convinced in this because I believe even up to this point in history that there have been many scientific, academic, and medical breakthroughs all because of revelation knowledge. I believe that Einstein and other inventors were under a prophetic anointing that caused them to excel and do things that hadn't been done before. In this book we have learned how throughout the history of the prophets, God raised up prophets or others through the prophetic to engage prominent spheres of culture and release the next moves of God.

The same is true of our generation. I believe we are next, and as a prophetic people, if we begin to infiltrate world systems, revival cultures will begin to emerge and set the stage for significant kingdom advancement. We are living in and are at the brink of the greatest move of God the world has ever seen in which a prophetic company of people will initiate according to Joel 2:28-32 and Acts 2:17-21. It's time we go back to the school of the Spirit so that we can be sure we are properly aligned for this next movement. You need to position yourself. What part do you play in this picture? What is in your house?

Made in the USA
San Bernardino, CA
10 September 2013